"Sanctuary! Sanctuary!"

"Sanctuary! Sanctuary!"

By DALLAS LORE SHARP

Essay Index Reprint Series

 BOOKS FOR LIBRARIES PRESS
FREEPORT, NEW YORK

INTERNATIONAL STANDARD BOOK NUMBER:
0-8369-2134-8

LIBRARY OF CONGRESS CATALOG CARD NUMBER:
73-128312

PRINTED IN THE UNITED STATES OF AMERICA

*To my friends
and the friends of all wild life*

R. J. H DeLOACH
and
FRED S. LODGE

Contents

"Sanctuary! Sanctuary!"

They shall not hurt nor destroy in all my holy mountain, for the earth shall be full of the knowledge of the Lord as the waters cover the sea.

"SANCTUARY! SANCTUARY!"

CHAPTER ONE: "SANCTUARY! SANCTUARY!"

*The high hills are a refuge for the wild goats; and the rocks
for the conies—when set aside by law and by law protected.*

JUST off the coast of Oregon, hardly a mile at
sea, rise three huge rocks, each pierced with
a wave-cut arch through which a small ship might
pass, and known for these great caverns as the
Three-Arch Rocks. The outermost rock is Shag.

On October 14, 1907, President Roosevelt set
aside this small group of unsurveyed islands as
the first wild-bird reservation on the Pacific coast
for the especial protection of sea fowl. But
things like this do not happen without a cause,
and seldom without a story.

Persons who are stories and who perform
stories, not imagine and pen them, often do not
know what a story is, nor what interesting tales
they could tell. That is true of Finley and Bohlman, who really stirred up President Roosevelt
to make a sanctuary of Three-Arch Rocks, the
beginning of a great work for the saving of wild

1

life in the Northwest. After much quizzing I have here the bare outline of their Three-Arch Rocks story.

It started when the boy Bohlman, the son of a coppersmith, met the boy Finley, the son of an undertaker, watching a bird in a tree along the streets of Portland, Oregon. That was years ago. And it was some years after this first meeting, when they were young men, that they chanced to hear of the rookeries of birds and sea-lions on Three-Arch Rocks and went to the coast to visit them.

On this first trip they could get no nearer than the shore at Netarts Bay. The distant glimpse they had of the rocks, however, the stirring of wild life on their craggy sides, and in the water about them, and in the air above their lofty heads, fired the imaginations of the young naturalists, and determined them to come again and actually scale the rocks in order to study the extraordinary wild life. That was in 1901.

Two years later, the young men were again on the shore of Netarts with kit and cameras for a prolonged stay. It was in June, at the beginning of the nesting season, and the sight offshore

about the three great gray piles of basalt was
more than their eyes could credit.

With their field-glasses they could see the herds
of sea-lions sleeping on the reefy ledges, the long
lines of black cormorants crawling by their wing
tips over the heaving sea, the colonies of white-
vested murres in stuccoed patches up the rugged
walls, the gulls like pearls against the basalt
brown, and now and then a tufted puffin, a mere
ball of black, hurled for some mark from off the
rocky peaks.

The only road to the rocks was by oars with
a boat. There were boats at Netarts and over
at Tillamook, but no man in either place who
thought so much of the useless birds and the lubber lions (which perhaps destroyed the salmon)
that he could be hired to make the trip to the
islands.

So the boys manned their boat, a fourteen-
foot dory picked up at Netarts. Neither of them
was a sailor, though of course they knew which
was stem and which was stern of the craft. Something more than that is helpful, however, in
handling a dory in the surf off the coast of
Oregon. Yet when a boy is bent on learning, it

is amazing how the waters teach him if he keeps afloat.

The surf was only part of the problem confronting them. There was trouble awaiting them at the islands, also. In order to make camp on the rocks they must have considerable equipment: fuel for cooking, a large supply of fresh water, tent and extra clothes for stormy weather, and food enough for a possible emergency. Here was a load. But besides this they had brought for work on the rocks an ample and a very heavy camera outfit.

It would require two trips to carry all of this to the rocks. But with no more than half of it the boys wondered how they were to drive their dory through the barrier of breakers pounding in upon the beach. Beyond the high-rolling surf lay the smooth, swelling sea, but across the stretch of that there was foaming water again on the knees of the arched rocks where they were to land. It was where to land, and where to stow their freight, and where to dock their five-hundred pound dory that perplexed the landsmen as they studied the abrupt tide line about distant rocks through their glasses from the shore. They must add a block and tackle to their already cumbersome kit.

Most men speed up under difficulties and do their safest work at greatest risk. The necessity for two trips was settled and the boys busied themselves wrapping their perishable freight in water-tight bags. As the landing might have to be made upon a narrow shelf of rock in the rise and fall of high-running waves, the weather conditions must be perfect. Only in a calm spell could one come under those precipitous cliffs with any kind of a boat, and a calm spell was not prevailing at that moment on the rocky coast of Oregon.

Though only about twenty years ago, this coming of Finley and Bohlman to the shores of Netarts was early, as education goes, in the history of wild-life protection. They were pioneers, breaking out a new attitude toward nature in their part of the world.

On their first trip to the coast, two years before, they had found a camp of sea-lion hunters on the mainland opposite Three-Arch Rocks. These hunters had a Columbia River fish-boat, a stanch seagoing craft, which they launched through the surf and rowed to the reefs two or

three times a week on shooting-trips, killing the
sea-lions for their hides and oil. The herds were
not large, and could not suffer that wholesale
slaughter long.

And quite as deadly as the camp of hunters
was a tug-boat, hailing from Tillamook Bay,
which during the summer made frequent shooting-trips to the peopled rocks. The owners of
the tug advertised openly, as sport, these shoot-
ing-parties, the "sport" consisting of the tug's
steaming round and round the rocks as close as
she dared to go while the "sportsmen" on deck
fired into the dense flocks of frightened birds
circling over their eggs and young and into the
diving herds of lions which they left dead and
dying in the heaving sea.

It is small wonder that for two years Finley
and Bohlman, realizing that something must be
done to stay this slaughter, and done quickly,
fumed at their enforced delay. At last their
boat was on the beach, and all was ready—for
they knew not what—except the weather.

The weather was threatening. A heavy fog
rolled like a bank of smoke upon the ocean westward, and hung in a rainy, slowly shifting cur-
tain from the peaks of the Coast Range out over

Three-Arch Rocks. So the boys pitched their four-by-seven tent on the shore, just out of reach of the breakers, prepared to wait, if necessary, until the morning.

Waiting proved to be very necessary. The long beach-combers were unusually high, and broke upon the sand in sets of three. A boat might ride one of them, but the second was timed so as to knock it hard, and the third would fill and crush it. And then three more were upon them! A fish-boat from the Columbia, in several hands and without a load, might be driven through and over the thundering wall, but not this laden dory. So they waited. And it began to rain.

I have seen it rain along the coast of Oregon. It is the rainiest portion of the globe, I think. Nine months of every year it rains, and those who live there say it is showery the other three. And this is because here the Coast Range mountains rise abruptly and hold back the sea. And the sea rises in its ancient fight against the land, pouring a continuous barrage of rainy storms against the flanks of the mountains, only to cover them from their feet in the breakers to their summits in the smoky sky with the deepest verdure, the mightiest, most glorious forests of fir in the world.

That old warfare was on as the boys crawled into their tiny tent away from the rain. The sea wind was very cold, and as twilight thickened upon the beach, the gusts shook their tent and growled like a herd of sea-lions from off the arched rocks.

Then night came. The wind freshened. Driving slants of rain slashed the canvas walls of their shelter. A wailing bird flew over now and then, but nothing clear could be heard above the pounding of the breakers on the shore. The mountain walls behind them gathered up the thunder, and poured it muffled down again upon the narrow beach. The earth beneath them trembled under the throbbing body blows, as if the mountains might themselves give way and slide upon them back into the sea.

So the long night passed, and never for a moment, as the two watchers lay listening, did they hear any lessening of the storm or detect a lost step in the mighty marching up and down the shore.

Morning came, and the rain rained on. At noon it was raining. It was still raining at night.

The wind continued as steady as the rain and the rolling sea. All day in the downpour the two boys paced up and down the beach, hoping for a moment's lull in the battle of the breakers, looking for gaps in the triple ranks through which with their loaded dory they might slip out to open sea. There was no lull, no breach, only a thickening of the fog as the second night blotted out their rainy world and drove them wet and shivering to their inadequate tent.

By this time the canvas walls were dripping inside, and even their waterproof beds were damp. The earth under their rubber blankets was saturated. Their clothes had not been dry since morning, and they got into their sleeping-bags as their only way of drying off.

Then morning came, and still the rain and wind and fog, and still the three great combers booming continuously on the beach. But at noon the sky suddenly cleared. The rollers broke with less thunder. Birds from the rocks offshore were moving overhead. The boys unloaded their kit and dumped the water from the dory, packed in their freight again, and made ready to shove off. By the middle of the afternoon, however, another southwest storm was brewing, and again the

night and the rain and the patrolling surf investing them in their water-logged camp on the
shore!

But they had had another glimpse of Three-
Arch Rocks that day, when the sun for an hour
burned off the fog, and the sight had dried every
particle of damp in their enthusiasm, whatever
the drip of their clothes, and sent them to sleep
with the purpose to pull off for the rocks in the
morning despite the surf and the murky sea.

They were stirring early, out into as cold and
gray and dank a dawn as ever a porpoise poked
his nose into. Though rapidly becoming amphib-
ian, they had not yet fully turned porpoise or
sea-lion; and so that day they exercised themselves, as on previous days, up and down the
beach, where the water was just as wet but not
so deep as seaward on the other side of the wall
of foam.

And so they watched and waited that day and
the next day and the next. For sixteen days and
nights they watched and waited for the sky to
clear and the heavy surf to give them a chance to
put off. That is a long time to be wet, and a very
long time to stand by your dory, oars in hand,
eager to dart into smooth, swelling waters where

clouds of crying sea-fowl and herds of bellowing lions are ready to give you welcome.

There is an end to all things, especially to human patience, if it be boy patience. They were going to the rocks whatever the weather; and, dragging the dory to the lowest place in the surf barrier, they waded in till the boat floated, then jumped to the oars.

A gallant little craft! And they were gallant lads. The nose of the dory plowed the froth of the first breaker, rose and stood poised like a gull on the crest of the second, and shot for the third like a flying fish.

Into the deep trough it headed, into a high green wall, and, leaping straight upward, reached for the curling top, when the giant thing combed. Crash! Half a ton of sudsy water struck the rowers, filled the little dory, knocked her endwise, when another monster caught her, and tossed her empty back upon the beach.

The remainder of that day was spent fishing out the cameras and other kit, and drying the precious freight. But the next day the boys were at it again, with exactly the same result, though with considerable damage this time to their provisions and delicate photographic things. This cooled them off a little, and they rested the next day, sure that there were signs of clearing weather.

The signs were real. The surf was lower, and, making ready the third time, with life, and something ever dearer, at stake, they faced the three foaming hurdles, cleared them, and rode into smooth water, with *cameras* for Three-Arch Rocks, not guns, with *life,* not death; the first to bring the gospel of our better mind to these wild brothers in the spindrift and continuous cavern thunder of their craggy home.

No, that is not the end of the story. It is enough, however, to show what mad stuff enthusiasm is, and how very certain both of these boys were to be drowned. How they managed to land that dory-load on the ledges of Shag Rock, the outer-most of the three, has never been explained to me. In 1912 I landed on the very ledge myself when it took one man to hold the yawl just off the reef as the waves rose and fell, another man to toss the tent, water-kegs and cameras, and a third man on the reefs to catch them in the air.

Land their load the two boys did, nevertheless, and, putting back to shore, brought off their second load, and successfully landed that. Then, dispossessing an old bull sea-lion of his bed, a lone outlaw from the herds, they scaled the wall, rigged their block and tackle, and hoisted the dory safely out of the clutches of the greedy sea.

Now they had arrived. And now the real story begins. What happened on Shag Rock during the next fourteen days would fill a book. Indeed, what happened the first day would almost do that. For I wonder whether anywhere else on the round earth there is such a concentration of wings and flippers and voices, of weaving, clacking multitudes on high; and in the clear green water below, rising all about your boat, such barking, bellowing herds.

Into this pandemonium plunged the boys with their tossing dory—into the clutch of the sunken reefs, into the dank, awesome shadows of the impending walls, into the noisome, guano-laden air, into the eddying currents and cross-rips of the chasms and canons, and into the cavern thunder, near, continuous, abysmal thunder, out of the sea caves, such as has ceased to reverberate elsewhere since land and sea were divided and creation brought to a close. Only creation never shall be brought to a close.

The three huge stacks of basalt rise close to-

gether out of the waves; and once beneath their
mighty eaves, once within the twilight and hollow
vastness of their portals, one is utterly shut away
from one's familiar world. Sizes are exagger-
ated; shapes are uncouth, fantastic, and goblin-
like, the blinking face of a bull sea-lion rising
within reach of your oar so human that you cannot strike it, though the monster might capsize
you, a fabled creature, real nowhere save in books
and in these resounding caves. The clangor and
tumult are confusing, and so alien, so menacing,
as to fill one with a sense of certain harm. But
this is largely the effect of the crowding, beetling
walls and their uncanny gloom.

They overhang upon you. The sky and the
wheeling sea-fowl are in sight above them, but no
glimpse of the top, no path along the sheer,
frowning faces, no landings; weathered shelves
for wings, but nowhere for a human foot to rest.
Far up the craggy heights in every seam and re-
cess nest the incrusting murres, their brown sides
and white breasts diminishing into points and
blurs of gray. And so many are the wings,
so great the lift of the ground-swell, that everything seems gone adrift, the Three-Arch Rocks

themselves, though hard aground, in danger of breaking up and toppling into the sea.

So far as the two naturalists knew they were the first to land on Three-Arch Rocks with the purpose of scaling them. Unsurveyed and unsubdued, without a known landing, and to all appearances without a niche level enough and wide enough to hold the four-by-seven tent, the rocks presented a picturesque, though not an easy, problem to the campers.

Working their dory around the inner rock, then around the twin-turreted middle rock, which offered nothing at all in the way of a foothold, the boys swung out beneath the towering sides of great Shag, past the rumbling arch, and riding the dangerous ground-swell, found themselves facing the open sea.

A low-laden dory is no craft for such waters. Without a port as yet, not knowing but they would be forced to return to the mainland, they felt their way along and came into a cove, somewhat protected by a half-sunken ledge thrust southward into the sea. Here at least was a landing; and though it might be awash at high tide, they saw a shelf about ten feet above them, over which an old bull sea-lion spilled himself, that might serve as dry-dock for their boat!

They drove down the blowing, protesting bull, standing well off themselves for fear he would swamp them when he struck the sea; and here, a piece at a time from the peak of the swell, threw ashore their two cargoes, cached them in several crannies farther up the wall, drew high and dry their dory—and wondered what might happen to them now, should another sixteen-day storm be brewing yonder behind the gray hill of the sea.

Speculations of this sort do not breed on Three-Arch Rocks, too much attention being required by hands and feet. Holding on is the absorbing occupation here. The boys now had to have a bed. They did not know that years later I should have to share it with them, spoon fashion; and consequently they softened up with drill and hammer a nubby space in a weathered rift hardly wide enough for two. Here on a pair of oars they leaned up their tent and were ready for the night.

Crowned heads might have found the couch uneasy, not the less uneasy at the thought of turning over; for if one turned freely and a bit too far, one would land on the snorting bull lion or, if it were flood-tide, in the billows, forty feet below.

When I tried the bed, I was disinclined to turn. One cheek for one night to a basalt mattress is all the law demands, and one side of your bony frame. You must save the other side for another night. Fourteen days on Shag Rock is a record for human endurance. It is their fourteen nights on Shag that entitle Finley and Bohlman to Three-Arch Rocks as a monument forever.

The experience of one of the nights, however, had romance as well as hardship about it. The wall above the tent ran straight up for about two hundred feet to a roof which slanted to a ridge-pole, dividing the great top from east to west. The south slope was burnt and barren except for myriads of gull and murre and cormorant nests; but the steeper, more shaded northerly pitch was covered deep with guano and supported a low vegetable growth.

On this north roof the droppings of the birds had accumulated in places to a depth of three and four feet, into which the tufted puffins burrowed and made their nests. Along with the puffins, sharing their entrances, the small Keading's petrels, much like our stormy petrels of the Atlantic, dig out side galleries and make their homes. The watery, yellow-flowered weed which has found it possible to blossom in the powerful soil gives just a touch of the earth we know to the wind-swept, fog-bound, sea-held rookery, on this pitch of the roof of Shag.

Few observers have studied the petrel's nesting-habits. While one of the pair broods, the mate is far out over the ocean for perhaps a twenty-four-hour flight. At least, they seem to return to their nests only at and after twilight, when they hover twittering above the doorways until their brooding mates come forth and waver furtively away.

In order to witness this strange coming and going the boys anchored themselves for a night on the eerie top of Shag.

It was a long, eventful watch, such a watch as brings one profoundly near the sleepless stars and nearer still to the scudding clouds and the beating wings. Over and again they heard the winnowing of the little petrel's marvelous wings, and listened to the hushed chitter as the tireless wanderer treading the air spoke softly to its mate as, wedged between outcropping points of the rock roof, to prevent their sliding, should they

chance to dream, they marked the silent passing
of the hours, felt the rumbling thunder of the
caverns, caught the wakeful night-talk of near-by
birds, and timed the throb, throb, throb of the
living sea.

High resolves and daring purposes come to the
clear minds of men in vigils such as these.

Fourteen days of the wild, incessant clangor,
fourteen nights of clinging like barnacles to the
wave-girt rocks amid the fetid odors of a million
sea-fowl, which all the winds of heaven failed to
blow away, had nothing dampened the spirit of
the boys. Their cameras had been busy till every
film was gone. Their food, too, was exhausted.
Their water-cask was empty. A gray and ominous bank lay seaward toward the south. The
soured old bull lion they had dispossessed was
barking at them to be off. And they were anxious to go.

Swinging their dory (they were practiced
now) from her rocky davits, they launched her
empty on a topping wave, loaded in their precious freight, and, pulling safely off, headed for
shore, making a solemn promise to the old bull
sea-lion, and to the flippered herds sprawling

along the ledges, and to the flying flocks that filled the air.

But none of the multitude heard it above their own raucous screaming, and none of them knew. They did not know how that vow took one of the boys across the States to the other ocean shore. They did not see the pictures of their rainy, sea-washed home spread in high excitement over a table in the White House, nor watch an eager man, all teeth and eyes and pounding fists, whanging about and bellowing: "Bully! Bully!" just like an old bull sea-lion. But Finley did. They did not see him study the pictures and vow, "We'll make a sanctuary out of Three-Arch Rocks." But Finley did. And Congress did.

And this was the solemn promise made by the boys to all their swimming, winging brothers, as they pulled away from the walls of Shag. For this was the cry of Three-Arch Rocks. Reef and rumbling cave and eerie crag and moaning sea winds had never, day or night, slacked in their stormy din, but with the bellowing herds and winging, wailing flocks, kept ever crying, "Sanctuary! Sanctuary!"

CHAPTER TWO: NOT TO THE SWIFT

The race is not to the swift
Nor the battle to the strong. . . .
But time and chance happeneth to them all.

Fighting is on between the English sparrows and my bluebirds for the box on the corner of the barn. Down in the orchard there is more fighting, sparrows, the same pair, possibly, against white-bellied swallows for an apple-tree hole, the sparrows in both fights losing, apparently, for the nests of the bluebirds and swallows go forward. This turn of affairs is due, I think, to the presence of a new fighter, the English starling, rival colonizer to his countryman sparrow, a bigger and better fighter. A pair of starlings have driven the flickers out of their ancestral home in the Baldwin tree, and now are on the Hill, hanging around the hickory where the flickers are building a new nest hole, in order to dispōssess them here.

These are local skirmishes in a great world war, not between bluebird and sparrow, or starling and flicker, but between man and nature. It started long before man was big enough to fight, but he is now the real storm center. Interloper, disturber, usurper, he seems to have had a very different place assigned him in the planet's original life-plan, so different as to make him look now in the scheme like an afterthought, a mistake made here by the messenger whose orders were for Mars. For he has grossly mishandled life, "broken Nature's social union," let the sparrow and the starling into the land of the bluebird and the flicker and the swallow to possess it.

The starling is a recent plague. Though not strong yet in numbers, it spreads like a plague, and already master of the English sparrow, attacks every other rival for his house and lands. The native birds have lived together happily until now, under an immemorial compact of nice adjustments and balances which the newcomer neither knows nor honors. The English sparrow has been in Hingham for seventy years, but still he is alien and has caused only strife in my bird world since he arrived. This starling is a stronger bird, more pugnacious, more domestic, too, in his instincts, and threatens greater damage. If unchecked, he will chase a thousand and put ten thousand native birds to flight. Hingham shall never fail doubtless of bird life, but she may know some day only starling life. These aliens, however fair, are a scourge, a false weight in the balance, brought from their native haunts and natural enemies to find neither let nor hindrance here.

It is interesting to see the adaptations of our native birds to meet the man-made exigencies of their lives: the swift from the caves and hollow trees taking to our chimney flues; the phœbe from the overhanging rocks to the bridge stringers and the coving of the house roofs, to say nothing of the pair that built for fourteen summers under my pigpen; the wild shy nighthawk, ghostly spirit of the woodland dusks, making shift to nest on Boston's tarry house tops; and more astonishing, the sight of a pair of small hawks swooping over the St. Louis Public Library this spring in the very heart of the city, and lighting familiarly as pigeons up under the cornice of a lofty building across the street from the Library! I am sure from their actions that they had a nest close to that jutting cornice. These are man-caused shifts, the direct result of his ruthless management of life, which must either bend or break short in his hand.

There is abundant proof that birds and men for the most part can dwell together if the birds are invited; and more and more as their part in human existence is understood, are they being invited, even a scant tithe of our stores being set aside for them; and for those that travel far there are provided aërial highways, states-patrolled, and paved by joint action of Canada and our own country. Yet this is a small step compared with the advance the birds themselves have made to meet their man-adjusted world.

We little realize how life is beset in its natural habitat; what a narrow foothold life often has; so much more are we impressed with the apparent margin to spare, the actual waste of life in Nature's hand. But this prodigality is her tragic effort to overcome Death's lead. All living forms compete in the great elimination races forever being run off; but when man enters as a contestant he breaks every rule of the game and "spikes" every dangerous rival. There is no umpire in Nature to rule him off the field.

The fight for life is closer than it appears. I have seen the August sky painted like a Turner

sunset with colors mixed of evening light and
floating pollen clouds.   Life had given the azure
heaven a wash of pure gold, had sown the whole
horizon with pollen, each particle pulsating with
life, a storm of vital dust drifting like fog across
the sky for fear some floweret might go unferti-
lized, some tiny ovule die untouched, and the
coarse race of ragweeds perish from the earth!
(Would this particular race of weeds might perish from Hingham!)

What if Nature thought so? What if she grew
indifferent, careless, and withheld her hand? She
knows neither coarse nor fine.   This very ragweed, dweller in waste places, fills the air with
pollen only because I have made so much waste
space in Hingham.   This weed under natural
conditions found life small and mean enough;
but let Aaron wave his devastating rod over forest and prairie, and comes the ragweed, tramp
of the waste lands, as out of Egypt, clothing the
naked fields with tatters, and leaving Aaron with
hay fever for his pains.

Sheer prodigality of seed has sometimes
stayed both time and chance till these inexorable
forces have been slowed to a standstill.   Older
than the hills is the sturgeon, coming down to our

day out of the primordial seas. Clad in armor
plate, it has stood off Death since the Devonian
Age, since before the reptiles wallowed in the
Mesozoic marsh, or even the rank ferns of the
coal beds flourished back in the Carboniferous
swamps. But Time and Chance are on its trail.

This is a new spring. The waters stir. And
into the Delaware out of its immemorial sea,
stems the elder sturgeon to spawn along the shallows of the river and bay. Some years ago I saw
a sturgeon towed into the fishery at Bayside, on
the Delaware, whose roe alone weighed ninety
pounds. Taking an ounce of this by the scales
and counting, I found the whole roe contained
about three million one hundred and sixty-eight
thousand eggs—a measure of the enormous odds
against this left-over life from the Devonian seas.

Gambling with these three millions of chances
against equal millions of hazards, Life has won
for the sturgeon for millions of years. But so
narrowly! Of these three million eggs (all of
these went into caviar), not more than three,
probably, would have escaped destruction and
developed into mature fish. The sturgeon hardly
holds his own; indeed, is steadily failing as a race;
rivers once alive with them at spawning time now

rarely visited; fisheries where caviar-curing since I can remember thrived as a business, now abandoned because the spring run of sturgeon has diminished or has altogether ceased.

A million deaths for a single life, and the sacrifice too small! It makes one think of human war.

And I stood upon the sand of the sea, and saw a beast rise up out of the sea, having seven heads and ten horns.

This is the creature John saw off Patmos. The beast one sees along this New England coast has a million heads, and more mouths than heads, and in every mouth a writhing sturgeon. Yet out of the mouth of the beast some have always escaped; but out of the hand of man not a sturgeon shall escape, nor a condor, nor a man.

From the sands of the sea, now climb the high Sierras; out of the swarming waters where the sturgeon spawn, scale the clear cold heights where the condor breeds. The condor, too, is doomed.

The American condor is the largest bird that flies. Instead of three millions of eggs, it lays but one at nesting time, and nests only every alternate spring. This single shell cradles the race. One helpless chick, wrapped for months after hatching in natal down, is life's single strand. But it has held, and still holds the glorious wings, suspending them above the Sierras as from a star. Over snowy Hood to San Jacinto south swung the sky course of the condor—until the white man came to California.

Now the creature is close cabined on the remotest Sierras and is seldom seen. He still lives, but I am watching to see him wind slowly skyward from his last lonely perch, and coasting westward, disappear.

Prodigal to meet the lust and savagery of the sea, Nature is as parsimonious where she can be as the sterile peaks in their passionless sun and air. Three million eggs for as many enemies in the sea, and a single egg here in the heights, and that two years apart; for here no enemy can approach, and even Old Age must climb for a century out of the canyon to reach the condor's crag. How thin and cold burns the flame of desire in this mated pair of the peaks!

Wings like the condor's need time to grow, and strength to meet the gales that share the heights, and room, vast room, above the mountain tops and through the courses of the clouds.

More than one young at a time might crowd the
starry spaces, while innumerable sturgeon fry
leave empty the hungry maw of the sea.

For weal or woe, the hand of man is upon the
world of all flesh. Many a cataclysm has overtaken it before: volcanic ash, and polar snows,
but never a force so destructive, possibly, since
time was, as the puny hand of man. And this is
so because the delicate balance in Nature seems
to have been struck without weighing him.

I have seen pandemonium break loose and
utter destruction at the mere presence of a man
in a sea-fowl rookery on the Pacific. Birds like
the herring gull and the cormorant, natural enemies, living side by side in safety, so nicely hung
the great rocks in Nature's even hand! But
when I stood among the nesting multitudes instant confusion reigned and death, the devouring
gulls swooping among the unprotected eggs and
young of the frightened cormorants with terrible
destruction. My presence alone in the rookery,
my mere being there, would have meant the end
of the cormorants.

How ragged the edge by which life wins I saw
last summer in my garden. For years I had
tried to time the hatching of the turtle's eggs,

but either I did not catch the turtles laying, or some keener student, like the fox, would spoil the secret before I arrived.

Last June, the fifth, I came just at dusk upon a painted turtle at the lower end of the garden, hollowing out a nest for her eggs. The ground had not been plowed for over a year, it was caked and stony, but the creature reckoned neither time nor effort, digging away unhurriedly with deliberate geologic action, reaching into the little hole with one hind foot after another in regular alternate turns, ten seconds apart by the watch. She worked with her hind legs only, resting on one, her shell canted sharply as the hole deepened, reaching in with the other leg for a footful of earth. This she gathered and kneaded into a damp little wad at the bottom of the hole; then rising from her canted position on the supporting leg till she could clear her loaded foot, she drew it forth, thrust it back of her, out straight its full length, and dropped the wad; pulled this leg back under her; lifted the other leg, pushed it down into the hole and repeated the operation —time after time until the nest was done.

I came upon her about seven in the evening. I lay down behind her and watched until nine, when one of my sons, along with the whippoor-wills, joined me. By this time the hole was as deep as her leg would stretch, and soon through the dusk we saw a white egg drop into the nest. Then two minutes later a second egg, a third, until seven were laid, an egg every two minutes with clocklike regularity. Then without stirring from her position, not even enough to dislodge a straw which had fallen across her slanting back, she began to cover the eggs, first one leg reaching back for sand, then the other, as if time were nothing, where the sun must mother, and the months must midwife, the hatching. She neither moved nor looked around to see the nest, or to see what sticks and stones she might be scratching in upon her eggs. A little tuft of wiry grass grew on the edge of her nest hole and this she reached for with both feet at once, catching it over and over, only to have it slip between her toes. It kept her covering a full half hour when, had she warped a point to one side or the other, she would have found her own little piles of soft sand.

At nine-thirty the mechanical creature was ready to crawl off, her nest covered even with the ground. I hurried to the barn, got a strong wire cage, sunk it well over the nest and weighted it with a stone. The foxes did not get this clutch.

That was June fifth. September twentieth I made this entry in my diary: "The turtle's eggs hatched to-day—one hatched. I have visited the nest almost daily since June fifth, and to-day one turtle lay feebly kicking on his back under the wire cage. I dug out the nest. One egg was infertile, one diseased, the young dying half developed; four eggs were fully incubated, but the young had died inside the split shells; one young one got out to the surface to tell the date of his hatching."

His eyes were shut; a long sharp horn still tipped his snout, by which he had ripped open the leathery shell of the egg; and he was utterly helpless. When tail and head were extended he measured one and one-quarter inches from tip to tip. After a week of nursing at the house he could paddle his own canoe, and I took him down to the stream. Of the turtle nests in my garden last year the foxes and skunks destroyed all but this one under the wire; and of the seven eggs one had hatched; and he was too weak to crawl to water without my help. Some do escape every

September or the race of painted turtles would have disappeared from my ponds. Let me lift my hand against them, and their end has come.

I know possibly the last wild pitcher plant in Hingham. There is many a swampy spot in Hingham which I hardly know, and many a pitcher plant in hiding, I hope, that I have overlooked; but this strange flower, once common in Hingham, will shortly disappear. One might even see it go, might with a single stroke, cause it to vanish and be known no more forever as wild and native here.

Fortunately, this species of plant is in no possible danger of extermination. Its range is wide and its swampy home a great protection. It is a hardy abundant plant elsewhere, but its struggle here is prophetic of so many fading forms that I can scarcely look upon this last lingering clump. A fearsome sight it is to see the passing of a race, the thwarting of a divine plan, the end of what had been intended for eternal years. Death we are used to, but not extinction. Here in the swamp is more than death: here is a race reduced to an individual, immortality putting on the mortal; the return unto the shapeless void of a form; the last spent pulse of a procreative power that started fresh from God when the world was young, as if God were dying in the swamp.

I drained the swamp, and that hurt. It also helped another plant, a common colorless sedge, which, pushing in from everywhere pushed the pitcher plant out—into the nowhere whence there is no return. Something that was, is not. One of earth's patterns has been lost. A pitcher has been broken at the fountain; a wheel broken at the cistern. We in Hingham shall never drink beauty from this well again.

Recently I stood looking into the asphalt pits at Rancho La Brea, California. I had held in my hand that morning an eight-inch tooth from this pit, the great curved fang of Smilodon, the saber-tooth tiger. The terrible weapon might have been torn from the tiger's jaw only yesterday, so perfectly had the impregnating oil preserved it. Thin, bladelike, its inner serrate edge pricked the skin and clung to the finger drawn through its scimitar curve. It was a perfect tooth. The beast possessing it had perished in his mighty pride. And here with him in the treacherous tar had perished two thousand of his kind. Skeletal parts of two thousand saber-tooth

tigers have been taken from this California tar
pool at La Brea.

As I stood by the pit I looked about me. Two
small ground squirrels watched me from behind
a eucalyptus tree; a forest of derricks rose over
against me, pumping oil; a stream of automobiles
whizzed past me on the paved road; but in the
pool below me the oily ooze bubbled thickly; and
below the ooze lay heaped the bituminized ends
of all the years. Geology here had scrapped her
later ages. This was Time's dump, the rendering
vat, where into nothingness and night a million
lighted days were smothered, and perfect forms
and lives!

What strange and mighty shapes have vanished here: tigers more dreadful than those of the
Amazon or Bengal, mastodons of monstrous size,
elephants, camels, tapirs, sloths, horses, dire
wolves, cave bears and bear dogs bigger than the
Kadiak bear, birds and reptiles without like or
kind among the living now—forever gone except
that their buried bones are found, and on those
rude and partial frames rough guesses hung for
what were once unique and breathing forms.

But new forms have taken their places? No,
not since the Pleistocene years. The panther has

taken the saber-tooth tiger's place, but the panther, a coward cat, was lurking in his den for fear of Smilodon. Not a new form has developed upon the earth since the fatal tar pools caught the last saber-tooth and smothered his terrible race. The earth had no more life then than now, but it had more shapes and races, more and greater!

We have seen some of those races vanish. We know the day and place when the last passenger pigeon died, when his kind whose seed was in himself, ceased to be. So with the Labrador duck, the Pallas cormorant, the great auk, the Eskimo curlew, the Carolina parakeet and at least five other American birds. These were here since we can remember; but they will never come again. Perhaps few if any of us in the East will ever see the California condor alive in his mountain home, or the band-tailed pigeon, or the white-tailed kite. Fate still pursues the wild life of California.

In Massachusetts have disappeared within the last fifty years the Canada lynx, the gray wolf, the black bear, the moose, the elk, the wild turkey, the whooping crane, the sandhill crane, and the black-throated bunting.

In a reservation on Martha's Vineyard, protected by a special warden, are the last score of living heath hen, a beautiful species of the grouse, once common all over the Eastern states. Here they barely hold on. The drift is too strong against them. They are too fair. Fate has marked them, and every other bird as large as the quail, for her own. Cats are now the chief enemy of these heath hen, but the hunter has been. Say the best you can for the true sportsman, he and the hunter are out to kill. Lurking about the edge of the reservation is also the thief who bags a specimen quietly to sell to the museum makers. There is a price on the heath hen's head—a growing price as the score of them dwindle toward the vanishing point.

It is dismaying to count the causes making for the destruction of wild life, and how inevitable many of them seem to be. Since 1835 from the near vicinity of St. Louis, Missouri, forty-four species of native plants have utterly disappeared. A few new forms have come in to take their places, but the causes operating for the destruction in St. Louis are not operating for the spread of those extinguished forms elsewhere. What

works for destruction in St. Louis, works everywhere the same.

The wild leek, turtle head, innocence, ragged
orchis, creeping St. John's-wort, marsh St.
John's-wort, fen orchid, bunch flower, mock
bishop-weed, long-leaved stitchwort and stout
stenanthium have been exterminated by cultivation; cultivation and pasturing combined have
killed out the moonwort, yellow adder's-tongue,
meadow fescue, small pale-green orchis, and the
large twayblade; cultivation and vandalism
combined have done for the closed gentian,
showy orchis, royal fern and the grass-leaved
stenanthium; cultivation and drainage have together killed out the spike rush, prairie white-
fringed orchis and Clayton's fern; pasturage
alone has killed the fibrous-rooted sedge, the blue
cohosh, hairy-lip fern, black cohosh, large corral-
root, evolvulus, white gentian, stiff gentian,
Michaux's leaven-worthia, false beech drops,
nodding pogonia, Engelmann's sorrel, lyre-
leaved sage, rock salaginella and spiderwort;
pasturage and vandalism have eliminated the
large yellow lady's slipper and the crested coral-
root; vandalism alone has exterminated the wood
lily; the Missouri River has washed away the

bearded day flower; the removal of sand on which the plants were growing has killed out the green adder's mouth and the gray polypody; the expansion of the city has destroyed the hawthorn and the American feather foil. Specimens of all these plants are to be found in the herbarium of the Missouri Botanical Gardens as members once of the local flora.

I cite this long list of the dead and how they died, to show that the battle still goes on, and that it is fierce and fatal. From the tar pools of the Pleiocene times to my own small day in Hingham, the race has not been to the swift nor the battle to the strong. Time and Chance happen to them all, with all the odds in favor of the alliance. Beaten back by Time, outwitted by Chance, Life hurls one line of shock troops after another into the fight, holding her unconquered front behind the deep-piled dead.

This is a warm April day, and down in the village of East Weymouth the stream called Herring Run is writhing with a new birth. Thousands of alewives are flapping up the shallow water to lay their eggs in Whitman's Pond. The purpose of the creatures is almost terrible to behold, their fight to reach the birth stool, to

spread their spawn thicker than the stars of the
Milky Way around the margins of the pond.
Nature groans in perpetual travail. Annually
the herrings come in from the safety of the deep
sea up this shallow path to the dam, where human
hands lift them over—a few of them, but take a
staggering toll. None of them had got beyond
the dam, and the race had perished here a century
ago, except that the town had provided for this
remnant in giving the iron mill the right to build
the dam. What does an iron mill reck of a run
of bony herring?

Where once the saber-tooth tiger and the
mastodon roamed, the cave man now bravely
runs at large and is wise to escape the tiger and
the tar pools! But he is himself a tar pool. And
for wild life he is the most treacherous and
deadly of all deep pits. What has he done since
yesterday about St. Louis? Here in Hingham
the last big holly tree was hacked down a little
while ago for a few green leaves and glowing
berries high in its scanty top. The pitcher plant
will go,[1] as the Weymouth herring would have

---

[1] Since that was written this particular ("last") pitcher plant has
gone — close search revealing no trace of it.

gone, had not the town provided a fish way into Whitman's Pond.

What has been going on at the dam in Herring Run must needs go on in Hingham and in St. Louis and in every valley and mountain in California, even out to the islands of the sea. The sole help of many a struggling wild form from now on will be my help and your help. Since the beginning man has been, and for a long time may be, on the side of Time and Chance, against wild life. But the better man must prevail over the worse, the lover of life and beauty over the destroyer, the wise economist over the greedy, short-sighted waster; and this finer, wiser man will give to the polar bear, to the pitcher plant, to the mighty condor, his Arctic Circle, his Hingham meadow, his Sierra range for a perpetual home. He will go farther: he will plant and propagate, as well as protect, and bring back to the bluffs and bottom lands about St. Louis the forty-four that have folded their beautiful tents and silently stolen away—unless they have crept to the edge of the Pit and into that primordial pitch whence there is no return.

> "Still glides the stream and shall forever glide,
> The Form remains, the Function never dies."

The poet should have taken a longer look backward—up the ancient river beds of geologic time. No ripple of water for ages here, the forms of the rivers gone, the functions also passed away. This very hilltop where I live on Liberty Plain, the high portion of Hingham, was once a vast glacial lake. A tiny trout stream that the fisherman steps across is all that now remains.

I have seen a river disappear, the Owens River, into the mouth of an aqueduct to be carried in the concrete walls across the laps of valleys, on the knees of mountains, hundreds of miles to a multitude of meters in Los Angeles, a river no more, the form blotted out, the function utterly changed. This the puny hand of man has done, this and more, for this hand makes rivers where there were none, and inland seas. Some day the weak hand will blast a highway for the sea winds through the high Sierras, letting their rainy wings overshadow Owens River Valley and Deep Springs Valley and Eureka Valley, even hover Death Valley, as the east winds from the Atlantic these April days will hover hill and valley here in Hingham until the parched winter land becomes a pool and the thirsty land springs of water. Such are human hands. "We can de-

stroy this temple and in three days build it
again," they say, laying hold on mountain, and
isthmus and plain. But the hands of Nature
more: they rock the ocean out of its little cradle,
they stay the sun, and toss to and fro the fixed
stars. The whole history of the earth is but a
series of cataclysms, tearing down and building
up—leveling the great races both of crag, and
bole, and bone. Like the worn-down hills, Life
has been worn down, pushed back and back again
to the edge of the pit from which each time es-
caping, she crawls back bereft of megatherium,
or archeopteryx, or mastodon, or smilodon, or
dire wolf or dodo, or passenger pigeon. The
greatest of the earth lie buried there, and some of
the loveliest, too.

Let man and nature join hands in common
destruction of life, and with our own eyes we may
see take place what heretofore only the eyes of
ages ever saw. Recently in the Missouri Botanical Gardens at St. Louis I was shown a pair of
cycads, a species of palm, male and female,
Macrozamia Moorei, from Australia. Because
the fronds of Macrozamia contain a poison
which causes paralysis in cattle feeding upon it,

the ranchers of Australia have warred upon it to exterminate it, and so nearly have they succeeded that the four specimens in the Missouri Gardens may now be the only plants of the species left on the earth. These were snatched from the burning—or the poisoning, for the plant is killed by chopping a notch in the trunk, then boring a hole to the center and filling it with arsenic. The director of the gardens told me he had heard of the approaching end of this old form and, sending to Australia, was so fortunate as to get what may prove to be the last four survivors of the race. This may be too late to save them for the future. How under glass and in a strange land can these venerable obsolete forms be multiplied and longer preserved? And to add to the tragedy of another vanished race, this particular cycad is thought to be "the only living link between the cycads of to-day and the Bennettiales, a group of fossil cycad-like plants existing in the Mesozoic Era," ages before the tigers were tangled in the tar of the La Brea pools. This hoary palm, somewhat like a giant pineapple, is two feet through the stem, with waving fronds twenty feet in the air!

How long and alone its stand against slow out-flanking Time! But how swift and sure its fall before the ax, the auger and the arsenic of Chance!

The human race is old but as a race less ancient by ages than this ancient cycad. Still we men have held out long enough against Time and Chance to prove that we are a vital and a valiant race and that we can prevail. But our fight is also against principalities and powers. Our own hands are against us. The last great war was not between nations but between Man and Life. It struck hard at human life; the ax hacked through the human rind; the auger bored into the human core; and now in the foolish hands of men is the poison, quick and deadly, to do for the wounded race what the cattlemen have done to the wounded *Macrozamia* whose royal fronds had so long crowned the wide Australian plains!

Arm for another war? Tigers! The race is not to the swift nor the battle to the strong. We cannot arm nation against nation any more, but only human life against itself. The saber-tooth tiger was armed—but not against the tar pool. Our men on the war front were more terribly armed than the tiger, but not against gas and germ and hate. Oh, the pits, the asphalt pits of war! How full of arms! War is the tar pool of human life, out of which, however armed, the human race shall not escape in the end.

CHAPTER THREE: MY TWENTY-FOUR DOLLAR TOAD

PROBABLY my toad would not fetch twenty-four dollars on the auction block. I certainly did not pay twenty-four dollars for him; nor am I advertising him for sale at that price. He is not mine to buy and sell, being mine only because he lives in my stone wall by the steps. If he belongs to anything it is to the place—the wall, the yard, the garden, and the sky and the stars, his companions through the night.

He is not so free as the winds to come and go, but he is as free as his slow squat legs can make him. This price is put upon him by the biological department of the government, as a measure of his value. This is a fair price, and an easy sort of arithmetic. There are men who can count in dollars and in no other terms.

As for me, I don't like the dollar-and-cent talk about toads and birds. There are other ways of valuing things than by the dollar mark.

With my toad, however, it is interesting to

have his practical value figured out exactly. I have always known him to be a useful citizen, but now that I can be taxed, possibly, for every toad in my garden, I certainly am going to guard him jealously.

But I should like to do a little hop-toad figuring with a pencil of my own. The man who figured this twenty-four-dollar value out didn't have a garden. That I am sure. He arrived at this figure with the help of reports and statistics. Those things cannot tell the truth, at least not the whole truth.

In my garden, among many other things, I have eighteen hills of watermelons, three vines to the hill. One cutworm, in one night, could destroy the three vines in any hill. But a big brown toad goes up and down and over and across that melon-patch every night catching cutworms. Suppose each night he catches the cutworm that had plotted to eat off the three vines in one of the melon hills. How much would I owe that toad at the end of the watermelon season?

Let me work that problem out, for no one else can do it, because no one else knows how much a watermelon costs me. I can buy one at the store for a dollar. But that's a store melon. You can't compare a store melon with a home-grown melon. The home-grown melon is very much higher in quality. It is also very much higher in price. I don't believe anybody knows exactly the cost price of a home-grown watermelon in Massachusetts. Perhaps twenty-four dollars. Perhaps more.

Say it is an average of twenty-four dollars each that a watermelon costs in my garden, and that each of the three vines in each of the eighteen hills, thanks to the watchful toad, bears one melon. That makes fifty-four melons, which, at twenty-four dollars each, come to $1,296.00— the tidy little sum I owe at the end of the watermelon season to my toad.

Now there may be an error somewhere in these figures. I may have selling price and cost price mixed up here. Certainly I should hate to sell one of my home-grown watermelons for twenty-four dollars. They are beyond price, so much labor, and love, and waiting, and disappointment enter into them; and often so little juice and sugar and core that I couldn't give one of them away, to say nothing of selling it.

These sums, I say, may not be wholly correct. Something must be allowed for what the scientists call *the personal equation.* A scientific toad may be worth precisely what the scientists say he is. But my toad is a personal toad—that's a different toad altogether, and a different price. And so with melons, and a whole world of things.

My farmer brother in New Jersey was at work in his sweet-potato patch lately when he accidentally got mixed up with a toad and a very doubtful affair.

The rows of sweet-potato hills were highly ridged, and as he was hoeing the young vines he noticed a large hog-nosed adder snake coming up the valley between two of the rows toward him. The snake was plainly looking for something. Its head was slightly raised, and if it had been a dog, he would have said it was sniffing the wind for some scent.

Do snakes hunt by scent? That is a question I should like to have answered, for surely this snake seemed to be so hunting.

Swinging forward with the sinuous motion of the gliding body, the head of the creature moved about on the level of the ridged rows, now along one row, then over to the other, when suddenly it rose a little higher and hung motionless and poised.

The snake was surely hunting. But was it now listening, or had it caught the *scent* of its prey? And what prey?

Man and snake were face to face and less than the length of a hoe apart; but the yellow eyes of the adder saw nothing—nothing more than a shadow, nothing for alarm. Something nearer to it than the man held its half-sprung body stiff in the air with attention.

Slowly gathering its length together, the snake, satisfied that it was right, deliberately thrust its shovel-like nose into the sand under one of the potato hills, until its head was buried to the neck, when, *flop!* and out on the opposite side of the hill tumbled a big toad who made off down the furrow as if Death were after him.

And Death was after him. Instantly the adder pulled out his head, went over the ridge, and, apparently picking up the scent, started swiftly on the hot trail.

The toad had lost no time getting off his mark, and, before the snake was well under way behind him, had taken a good twenty hops, climbed the steep ridge of hills, and dropped out of sight in the furrow on the other side.

Nor had the snake yet seen him. And this is

what makes it seem the certain work of the reptile's nose, for without the slightest hesitation the
adder, like an awful fate, was in pursuit, going
back down this row. Coming to the point where
the toad had climbed the ridge, the snake climbed
over also, and into the furrow, reversed himself,
and now came once more up the row toward my
brother, the toad in sight and losing ground at
every hop.

The man through all the little tragedy had not
stirred a muscle. On came the frightened toad,
going as probably the short, dumpy thing had
never gone before, straight at my brother. It
landed by his feet, took another feeble hop, and
dived between them, just as the hungry adder
got within striking distance of the long hoe.

Few men in the face of a snake think twice before they act. There was a flash of steel in the
air and the chase was over. The adder literally
bit the dust, as its habit is when hurt. The toad
hopped on in safety, while my brother went
about his hoeing, twenty-four dollars saved, if the
Biological Survey is correct, but very much out
of pocket as an observer, and still more as a
philosopher, for his hasty act, wondering what
right he had to kill the snake, and if he had not

made matters worse instead of better in his small
world of reptiles and toads and sweet-potatoes.
I have a feeling that he did make matters very
much worse. It is just a feeling. The toad is
doubtless worth twenty-four dollars. I do not
know how much the snake is worth. But I have
a feeling that he, too, is worth twenty-three or
twenty-four dollars, though I cannot "prove" it
as I used to my answers in arithmetic. This is
a kind of "profit and loss" problem. Those in the
arithmetic were hard enough. This one is harder
than any there.

For who knows enough to say: "This toad will
bring me profit. This snake will cause me loss.
So I will spare the toad and reap the profit; but
I will scotch the snake and avoid the loss"? A
man's world is bigger than his sweet-potato
patch. Most things have many values, but there
are few things so highly priced as life. A dead
snake is worthless truly. Can this be possible
also of a snake's life?

Yesterday I bent down a walnut sapling along
a shady street in order to peek into a red-eyed
vireo's nest. Behold, one vireo egg and three
eggs of the cowbird! I took out the three evil

cowbird eggs and told the young boy who was with me to destroy them.

I saved one good vireo at the cost of three bad cowbirds. Who says "good" and "bad"? To-day in my neighbor's meadow I watched a little band of cowbirds feeding about the noses and under the very feet of the cattle, hopping up and settling close to the Ayrshires as they grazed slowly along the stream. If cattle could observe and write what would they say of good vireos and bad cowbirds?

On the road to the village is a well-kept garden, open to the rain, sloping toward the south, of warm, sweet, mellow soil in perfect tilth, a lovely, living thing, the joint work of human hands and hands within the earth and from the sky. In the middle of the garden, like a felon from a gibbet, swings the mummied body of a crow.

It is a black thing—blacker than its raven feathers; stake and string and dried distorted wings the sole work of human hands. The bird had come to the garden in the spirit of the sun-shine and the rain, a helper straight from nature to get the beetle and the grub. But he had also helped himself to the sprouting corn.

Hang him head down in the middle of the garden! Publish to every passing crow that this shall be his fate, also, should he venture under the open sky within gunshot of the garden! And publish to every passing man along the street that this is a human garden, a garden with a gun as well as a hoe.

However good the corn crop in that garden, there is something evil growing there. A hedge of hollyhocks and old-fashioned flowers incloses the garden, but the black thing on the gibbet darkens their bright faces and leaves all the glory stained. The blessing of Heaven is on the hoe, but on the gun is the curse of Cain.

There must be a better way. After planting my corn I hang a wide shingle from the top of a slanting stake in the garden, the string run through the *thick* end, the thin end free to spin and toss in every breeze. The crows never pull my sprouting corn. Except for stealing a few sweet cherries, which chance to ripen just as the young crows get a-wing, the crows from corn-planting time to melon time do only good to my garden, and no suspicious shingle turns in the wind, once the corn is well up, to warn them away.

It is hard to walk upon this green earth without stepping on the grass. There is so much grass. So is it hard to plant a little garden in the wilderness and keep the wilderness out. Cat-like, round and round the thatched village creeps the jungle, ever trying to get in. We invented the gun to help stand it off, but the older, simpler, more effective tool is the hoe. Heaven can be brought to earth by hoeing; it is desolation that follows the gun.

Nevertheless, the crow and the cowbird and the snake are problems, while it seems quite certain that I have a twenty-four-dollar toad. The other night as the car climbed Mullein Hill and the search-lights swept the dooryard and flashed into the open barn, there on the barn-door sill sat my toad, directly in the path of the wheels, staring blindly into the glaring lights.

Pulling up short, I waited for him to hop off. One is not going to run over a twenty-four-dollar toad if one can help it. A little knowledge, an old adage says, is a dangerous thing, but not if it is as much as twenty-four dollars' worth. That one bit of knowledge got hold of by the public about the toad would greatly increase the lowly batrachian's margin of safety. If the public could get hold of still more knowledge about the toad, about his soulful singing in the spring, his strange homing instinct, his extraordinary habits —drinking through his skin, eating up his old clothes—the public would find him even more interesting than he is profitable, and so make his humble place in the dooryard and garden both beautiful and secure.

"Ugh!" exclaimed a very *nice* little girl, "he is so bunchy and squashy and big-mouthed and homely!" So he is. He is not a bit like a butterfly. Nobody would mistake him in the garden for a pink or a pansy. Call him ugly if you dare to, but don't let the fairies hear you. For the toad is a fairy, if you only knew. If not a fairy, he is a goblin, a good goblin, and only missed being a fairy by a margin of wings. He has lovely bow legs instead—on the front; and a horizontal pair behind.

Goblins gobble and fairies are fair, and there is a great difference in that. Let evening come, and the day's work be finished, and the soft twilight creep down over the garden, then who shall guard the tender lettuces and the sprouting beans? We house-folk will soon be fast asleep.

With the dusk comes the dew, and together they creep beneath a little melon-vine and whisper: "Wake up, sleepyhead, and wink the dirt out of your eyes. The hoe-man has gone. The cutworms are crawling, and a bushel of bugs are marching on the garden. Wake up!"

Then the earth heaves, cracks, and falls away, uncovering a big pop-eye which blinks laboriously once at the damp and once at the gloom. This exertion leaves everything at a standstill. The wink takes place again. Then the standstill takes place for another extended time. But now the soil is bulging, breaking, and, as you live, a clod of earth with eyes and legs is emerging! Or is it a troll?

A troll it is, if ever there was a troll, a dwarf, droll troll, squat and humped and warty. And off he hops with the earth of his bed still sticking to his back. Then he stops to look and listen! But not to look at the fireflies sputtering over the garden, nor to listen to the whippoorwills whimpering in the wood lot.

Something is moving in the lettuce row! Something small and still, so still that a hoeman's ears could never hear it. The goblin troll turns his head, stretches his baggy body till it is taut, that he may the better hear. Then he turns the rest of himself around, takes a step, a hop, a jump—and flash! Out shoots a long tongue and in it shoots, and the cutworm shoots in with it. And the less we say about that cutworm, the more we can say about the lettuce.

Up and down the lettuce row, up and down the bean row, up and down the onion row, up and down the radish row, up and down the tomato row, up and down and over and across the rows and rows hops the good goblin, missing more grubs and bugs than he finds, I am sure, but finding enough to keep the garden safe till daylight comes, and the hoe-man comes to carry on.

In the beet row a dozen baby plants lie withered on their sides. "A cutworm!" growls the hoe-man. A little squash-vine is wilted. "The striped beetle!" fumes the hoe-man. A stalk of tender corn looks curled and sickly yellow. "The horrid borer!" swears the hoe-man, scratching the ground like a chicken, his foot within an inch of a melon-vine under whose shelter, buried out of sight in the soil, sleeps the good goblin.

The goblin's round little belly is bulging with cutworms and striped beetles and borers. The goblin is very comfortable and, like *Joe, the fat boy,* is very sound asleep. If the man with the hoe could count all the ingredients of the goblin's comfort, and the numbers, then reckon the numbers of beets and onions and melons and lettuces still standing in their rows, until he had the exact equivalent of the goblin's contents, and could reckon their value in terms of the green grocer, he might find the good goblin was sleeping off about twenty-four dollars' worth of vegetables, taken as concentrated insects in a single night!

That, at least, is the way I figure it, being a gardener.

CHAPTER FOUR: THE WILDNESS OF BOSTON

*"And that is why the faithful gale
Round Park Street Corner still must blow
Waiting for him with horns and tail—
At least, some people tell me so"—*

THE DEVIL, according to legend, having vanished through the doors

"In yonder church on Brimstone Corner,
Where pleasure's dead and lacks a mourner,"

leaving the gale, his naughty companion, to play outside and wait for him who should never return.

Perhaps Boston is no windier than any other city, than Laramie, Wyoming, but it seems so. It is certainly a weatherful city. So are the cities of Florida and California, where people live by the weather. We Boston folk live in spite of our weather. It is perfectly natural that one of the first and best weather stations to be established in this country should watch over Boston from the top of the Blue Hills of Milton.

No one who wears clothes in Boston is for a

single day in doubt as to what time of the year
it is. Not that our merchants capitalize the
weather as weather, after the fashion of Palm
Beach and Los Angeles, where it is the chief
article exposed for sale. Weather is a phenome-
non in Boston, and is turned devoutly over to the
Transcript, and made the subject for editorial
meditation and prayer. There is a certain pietis-
tic touch still manifest in our attitude toward
nature, an inheritance from the time of Mather
and Wigglesworth:

"Now farewell, world, in which is not my treasure,
I have in thee enjoyed but little pleasure—"

probably done in March. Mark Howe's faithful ballad,

"The Devil and a Gale of Wind,"

could not have been written outside of the streets
of Boston.

Boston smells all over of the sea—the sea of
the sacred salt cod rather than of commerce, for
those who go down in ships from Boston seem
fishermen, mostly. Big transatlantic boats come
and go, but no one sees them, no one smells them,
no one cares, for they do not affect the price of
cod. Yet Boston is nothing like so wharfish and

fishy as Gloucester. Outside of Dock Square and the leather district, there hover the faint odors of wool and hay about Boston. She is rural and ruminant. How pasture-like you never realize quite so much as when you are fresh returned from New York or Chicago.

The roomy, open Common goes far down toward the leathery belt of things. The Public Garden opens into a wide avenue, which runs straight (at least in the case of this one street) for several blocks out to the Fens, where the edge of the country begins. Suppose you do have to cross a river, the Mystic, or the Charles, or the Neponset, in order to enter Boston, or else come up the bay with the tide and the Grand-Bankers? You can stand on Beacon Hill, when the wind is right, and almost sniff the celery in the fields of Arlington, and almost hear the roosters crowing off in Hyde Park.

I can walk clear across Boston one way, from T Wharf to the border of Brookline, in an hour's time; but starting on the Milton side of Boston, I can keep going all day, through Matapan, Roxbury, Jamaica Plain, Cambridge, Somerville, Everett, Malden, Melrose, without seeing the opposite edge of the city, not the city politically,

but commercially, that continuous peopled plain
of which old Boston is but a fractional part in
area and population.

Here are the makings of a really vast city, yet
no one gets an impression of interminable streets,
such as one feels in Philadelphia. No street
seems to run very far in Boston. It is sure to run
into itself or into a harbor or a basin or a pond
or a park or into a nice old graveyard where
birds, and the ghosts of yesterday, make their
nightly roosts.

The bays and beaches on the seaward side; the
rivers, ponds, low-lying meadows, and the rocky
heights, like the Fells and the Blue Hills Reservation, on the landward side about Boston, give
it a wilder setting, and divide it more with nature,
than is the case of any other city of its size I
know.

From my upper windows in Hingham I can
read, with my field-glasses, the time on the clock
in the Custom House tower in Boston, yet the
red fox and the white-tailed deer are frequent
visitors of mine; the skunk, the weasel, the rabbit,
the mink, and the muskrat are regular inhabit-
ants of my immediate fields and swamps.

On the ledgy coving about the lofty top of that

Custom House tower, looking down upon Fanueil Hall Market and the harbor, a duck-hawk makes his winter home. He is the most daring of our birds of prey, the famous peregrine of falconry, from whose swift wing and terrible talon the speediest flier has slender chance of escape. A lonely bird, dwelling on inaccessible crags, near the water, remote from man, he has chosen the tall tower of the Custom House for his hunting, and here, above the tumult of the busiest mart in Boston, looking far down upon the huddled streets, the fierce wild creature watches for his prey, swooping now upon some flying pigeon, now, like a meteor, with half-closed wings from out the clouds, striking a wild duck on the surface of the harbor—come and gone, back to his granite crag above the weaving ways of men far down on the narrow streets below.

The wild life of my Hingham Hills is renewed from the Blue Hills of Milton. Counting the wild-life reservation of the Blue Hills (which is a part of the metropolitan park system) as technically a part of Boston, we can say that all of the animals about me here in Hingham, and

many more, including the rattlesnake, are as
truly Bostonians as any Cabot or Casey.

Species for species, the wild things of Boston
can be matched, perhaps, in any other city. Indeed, New York's Central Park is a better warbler country in migration time than the combined Common and Public Garden in Boston.
As most birds migrate by night, the very lights,
and the vast extent, of New York City draw
down the migrants from a wide roadway in the
sky, Central Park offering them a better, because a bushier and more varied, shelter, to rest
in over the day, than our Common and Garden.

But the wildest thing in Boston is its mind.
And I wonder if that natural mind can be paral-
leled in New York or anywhere else. Boston
thinks and feels not wildly, but—naturely, may I
say? If by taking thought, by building a jutting
ledge from the tall tower of the Custom House,
Boston could induce a duck-hawk to bring its
mate and breed here, I think the city would ask
the architect to incorporate that detail in his
plans, and thus would dedicate the structure
jointly to business and to birds—to *Falco pere-
grinus anatum* so long as he observes all the com-

mands of the Society for the Prevention of Cruelty to Animals to do them.

Among the religions of Boston Common we must give a place to bird-worship. Forty years ago Bradford Torrey, in a chapter called, "Birds on Boston Common," set forth the doctrine. Here on my desk lies a volume published in 1909 devoted to the *Birds of the Public Garden,* the garden being not quite so holy a temple as the Common, but better attended by the birds.

Boston worshiped at the shrine of nature long before Bradford Torrey became high priest. Not since the days of John Josselyn's *New England's Rarities Discovered* in 1677 has the religion of wild life been without a minister in Boston, or the minister without a congregation. What other city has had an outdoor training by such a group of teachers as Boston's poets and naturalists? While not of the actual parish, all of them, yet all of them are of the congregation, though as far away as Concord and Portsmouth. Whatever is in New England on the east side of the Connecticut River, except Rhode Island, is in Boston. Here all the tracts and sermons of the over-souls were published, here listened to and discussed.

If Boston has a wildish mind is it not reasonable after the ministry of Emerson, Thoreau, Agassiz, Longfellow, Flagg, Gray, Lowell, Nuttall, Angel, Torrey, Maynard, Higginson, Minot, Pope, Forbush, Baynes, and Packard? And what other city has created and sustained an *Atlantic Monthly*? Ever since Lowell edited the first issue it has been instructing Boston in ornithology, conchology, entomology, and wood lore generally. In the *Atlantic* appeared Emerson's "The Titmouse" (a bird, kind reader), Whittier's "Telling The Bees," and Holmes's "The Chambered Nautilus." For sixty-two years John Burroughs contributed his outdoor papers to the *Atlantic*. And for some of those years the *Atlantic* hardly circulated outside of Boston and her purlieus!

Bradford Torrey tells of meeting a business man on one of the crowded streets of Boston. "Ah, good morning!" Yes, he was very well. "And yesterday I saw my first fox-colored sparrow and heard him sing!" Probably that is nothing unusual in Chicago and Philadelphia. It certainly is a very characteristic thing in Boston.

One of my friends, blue-bred since the days of the slave and China trade, an honored woman of many distinctions, was recently ascending the subway stairs on the Common when she beheld a naked nestling on the stone step at her foot. She hesitated—and was lost. Shunting the jostling crowd, she snatched the helpless thing from the devouring feet and carried it out to the mall.

She was on her way to preside at some patriotic function—with this squirming infant in her hand! The afternoon throng surged back and forth as she stood there divided betwixt her presiding and her mothering, for the little beast had grabbed her finger with its long claws in a grip which strangely clutched her heart.

How could she drop it? But how could she preside with it? Then she bethought her of the bird-and-pet store on Bromfield Street, and waving back the traffic, she swept across Tremont Street and down to the bird-and-pet store in Bromfield Street inquiring, anxiously:

"Do you—do you have an infants' department —a crêche—a nursery here?"

"Yes, madam," said the bird-and-pet man, to her vast relief.

"Then I wish you would feed and tend this— this thing for me," laying the pot-bellied offspring of an English sparrow on the show-case, "till I can come for it next week." And she fled.

But the next week she returned to arrange for the foundling's future, only to find it already well provided for. The bird-and-pet man had been short on live worms, he told her, and so had fed the infant bred and milk for three days. Then it died. "And the combined bill for board and care and undertaking was only fifty cents," she told me. "An extraordinarily reasonable bird-and-pet man, don't you think?" she asked. And I said I thought he was.

For many seasons an old barred owl has been in the habit of making the Granary Burial Ground his winter home. I have often seen him there, as much of a show to me as Paul Revere's tomb down under the elms below. Lately complaint was lodged against his Wisdom for being unwise in his choice of roosts on certain window-sills.

The Animal Rescue League was appealed to. The league trapped him, and for two days tried its very kindest to feed him, but the old philosopher refused to eat. Then the league, alarmed, sought the Massachusetts Audubon Society for dietary instructions, only to be told that the case was hopeless, that the owl would die of his hunger strike. The league in its mercy then said it would chloroform him at once and have him mounted.

It was now the turn of the Massachusetts Audubon Society. By what authority would the Animal Rescue League take the life of this bird of prey? It was a useful citizen, protected by the laws of the commonwealth; and the Audubon Society took steps at once to stay the execution. Here was a case for the lawyers. And of course, being lawyers, they all got busy. And what was the verdict? His Wisdom was turned over to the Audubon Society, and taken by it into the far country, where his cage was opened in a dusky, roomy barn, known to be full of the choicest mice. Floating from his narrow wire cage up to a lofty beam, the self-starved Wise One, turning, looked down upon the Massachusetts Audubon Society with big, knowing eyes, and as soon as the barn was left to darkness and to him alone, drifted through the open door, and on wings that were shod with silence, made off into the freedom of the wide and starry night.

So does the city of the sacred cod concern itself. Such things could, and do, go on elsewhere;

but they are the order of the day in Boston, as much in her mind as cotton and wool and education and religion.

When I was a dweller on Beacon Hill (where the City Club now stands) my roof, between the State House and the Court House, was a regular and a profitable post for bird study. Some of the tops of the old English elms on the Common were in sight then, and what with the Common and the harbor and King's Chapel and Granary Burial Grounds, I was at the center, or at the zenith, rather, of a world of wild wings. Gulls, terns, geese, and ducks from the harbor were not infrequent voyagers through my sky, especially in the winter; and the spring migrants, and the regular summer residents, made the tall house-tops on Beacon Hill a landmark and a rendezvous.

I knew certainly of half a dozen pairs of night-hawks nesting among the tar-and-pebble roofs, behind the chimney-pots. But these particular birds are fewer now.

Brought up as a child by the river and in the edge of the deep woods, I was early impressed with the weird behavior of the ghostly-booming "night-jars," and to find them on my roof in the heart of a great city, years after they had ceased to call to me from above the shadowy woods, was like finding my youth again, and something more. There was but a single pair of chimney-swifts over Beacon Hill in those days, so far as I could see, though it was not for lack of chimneys, ancient ones and roomy.

The scarcity of the swifts was due to scarcity of food, I am sure, a factor in the distribution of bird-life which of late has worked some striking changes in Boston.

In April, 1903, I wrote of the famous sparrow-roost in King's Chapel Burial Ground: "Morning must have begun to break along near four o'clock, for the cold gray across the sky was already passing into pearl. The country birds had been up half an hour, I am sure. However, the old cemetery was wide enough awake now. There was chirping everywhere. It grew louder and more general every moment, till shortly the six thousand voices, and more, were raised in the cheerful din—the matin, if you please, for as yet only a few of the birds were fighting.

"To the clatter of voices was added the flutter of wings. None of the sparrows had left the roost. The storm of clatter increased and the buzz of wings quickened into a steady whir, the noise holding its own with that of the ice-wagons pounding past. The birds were filling the topmost branches, a gathering of the clans, evidently, for the day's start. The clock in Scollay Square station pointed to five minutes to five, and just before the hour struck, two birds launched out and spun away. The exodus had begun."

Along with the State House codfish and the Public Library lions, this sparrow-roost in King's Chapel yard was one of the wild wonders of Boston. Six thousand voices at least in the daybreak chorus; six thousand little bodies covering the naked limbs of the elms and the single honey locust like summer leaves for numbers; and when the winds blew and a great storm from the sea swept through the high-walled streets and bent the trees in the graveyard harbor, it was a stirring thing at midnight to see this fleet of six thousand tiny sail riding at anchor here, every wing reefed, every head battened down, every breast to the gale, while the very streets shrank into empty doorways and the tall lights blinked in the sleet and snow.

A few sparrows are roosting in the old burial-ground to-night, but the great flock has dwindled almost away. Not for a long time will the last sparrow disappear, yet the automobile will finally do for him. The sparrows cannot live on oil and gasolene. When the last horse is displaced, then the last little sparrow scavenger, who lived on the half-digested grains of the horse-droppings, will spread his wings, never to return to the ivy-covered walls of Boston, and the dying elms and the honey locust in King's Chapel Burial Ground.

The night-hawk and the chimney-swift are going with him, and later on the water-bug and the cockroach. But these have not yet wiped their feet against the sinks of Boston, nor have the mice and the wretched rats shaken off the dust of their feet against us. It is not surprising, then, that this last summer a pair of sparrow-hawks should nest on the Natural History Building in the Back Bay. Just where the birds hunted and upon what they preyed no one found out, nor how they managed to share the hunting-grounds with the many house cats of the city. But they handled the situation successfully until their nestlings were nearly ready to fly. Then the young flappers, catching the spirit of the city, got out on the street in their pin-feathers, and were taken up, sheltered in a benevolent institution, and there protected until they could use their wings.

There is nothing peculiar to Boston in this. I saw what I took to be the building operations of a pair of small hawks (sharp-shinned, possibly) in the heart of St. Louis recently; and a census of sixty-seven wild birds in a single day was taken some little time ago in New York City. What I wonder is, if anywhere else so many eyes see these things as in Boston, so many diaries record them, and if anywhere else they are so real a part of so many lives?

On my way home from Boston this January day I saw a man feeding the wild ducks along the Riverway. I nearly ran over a hen pheasant in front of the Arboretum. As I came out to the edge of the city, I met two interesting figures in hip-boots with long eel-gigs, on their way, I suppose, to the Neponset River. And on the ice of the Weymouth Back River, a bit out of the city, to be sure, I saw two tiny tents pitched, each housing a smelt-fisherman, whose lines were dangling through a hole in the frozen surface for the silvery little folk in the water below.

To travel on foot from T Wharf, where the fishing-boats come in, to Franklin Field and the city zoo is probably as rich a day's tramp for wild life as can be taken in the United States, notwithstanding the fact that last April I returned from an all-day hunt about Santa Barbara, California, with one hundred and nine species of wild birds to my credit. What Boston lacks in birds it makes good in fish.

It is the fish in the old Quincy Market, and at the wharves, which give unique meaning and a strictly Bostonian flavor to such a nature walk. Every strange creature that comes to the nets, or the lines, of the offshore fishermen finds its way to the market. I presume that the other bebundled saunterers whom I commonly meet among the stalls there come, as I come, to smell the smells and see the sights which the fishing-boats bring in.

Was it because I had the run of a shipyard as a boy, and all of the people of the village "went to sea," that the sight of a sail and the sniff of low tide roils the shallows of my civilization and stirs the elemental ooze at the bottom of me?

Boston is not a limpet or a lobster, though still a creature of the sea and the rocky shore, and

the greatest port for fish in the world. How
perfectly natural to find almost any day in her
market such a school as scrod, swordfish, red-
snappers, scup, squid, squeateague, sharks,
skates, smelts, sculpins, scallops, shad, and
sturgeon (in season)—just to mention the string
that begins with *s!* And what river-banks, what
shores and deep seas, what gear—line and net
and dory—what weathers, risks, and flags at half-
mast they all suggest!

We have a good aquarium in Boston, its cap-
tives from the deep, with slowly waving fin and
sculling tail, a strange, alien folk within their
watery walls, notwithstanding our familiarity
with the Georges and the Grand Banks. But we
can say little for our collections and museums,
the wildness of Boston being found in nothing
mounted or caged.

Boston has the least stuffed-animal and la-
beled-specimen interest of any of our great cities.
It is more concerned with the feeding of the
pigeons and the gray squirrels on the Common.
Compared with the Zoo and the museums of
New York, ours in Boston, not counting the
Agassiz Museum at Harvard, remind one of the
parable of the mustard seed. Yet what we have

is strictly to the purpose and complete after its kind—excellent local collections entirely for local ends. This city being the hub of the universe, finds the universal here; our very museums handling their collections of the things of Nature, as Thoreau handled Nature herself—"as if she was born and brought up in Concord."

I wonder what a New-Yorker would think if he should discover our Children's Museum in the Fens? Beside his American Museum of Natural History, this remarkably effective little thing in the Fens looks for size like a common shrew beside a sulphur-bottom whale—forty grains of mammal shrew up against one hundred and fifty tons of mammal whale! Some one has figured that it would require fifty-two and one half millions of shrews to bulk as large as one such whale. I wonder what New York would think of this museum of ours? I also wonder if this shrew of a thing in the Fens may not produce as much wildness in Boston, perhaps, as that whale of a thing produces in New York? It would be interesting to compare the numbers of children going and coming from the two museums directly into and out of the woods.

One of the losing-winning fights that nature

is ever waging with its sores, which we call cities, is going forward in the Fens of Boston, along the small margins of Muddy River, in what was once the salt marsh of the Back Bay. Here the plants of the sea-shore, long since cut off from their salty tides, are making a last feeble stand against the combined armies of the upland, the fresh-water, and the escaped garden forms, many of the latter not native to American soil. Only the trained botanist knows the full extent of this investing siege, and sees the silent battle receding into the fatal shallows of the little river.

But here is one plant of the shore that holds stoutly out against all comers, though only in two or three small clumps. That is what we used to call "green-head grass," *Phragmites communis,* a tall, plumed knight of a grass, from ten to twelve feet high, well known among the marshes southward. Here, with back against the wall, a meager remnant, gallantly, gloriously harnessed, still waves magnificently defiant.

In South Boston *phragmites,* besieged, seems to have made a more dramatic, indeed, a most extraordinary, defense, resorting to methods of modern warfare and digging itself in. For here, I am told, a form of the splendid grass has developed prostrate stalks, several yards long, and rooting at the nodes, as if, in the face of certain extinction, it had invented a new weapon, been driven by the extreme situation to resort to a new device, raised to a higher power by the overwhelming odds.

As everywhere in vacant city lots, dumps, and waste places, the conflict between native and foreign forms goes on in Boston's world of plants. The immigrants have so completely won in certain regions as now to be fighting among themselves for a place in the sun. A gorgeous warfare wages along the shores of the Neponset River between the yellow tansy and the white *melilotus* (sweet clover) for complete possession of the land. As a bee-keeper, I wear the white spike of melilot, for it is a wonderful honey plant, though tansy's good for tea.

And while they war, witness, will you, the azure triumph of the common chickory! There are weeks along Brook Road made glorious by the chickory, when the ride that way to Boston is worth while just to pass through the skyey stuff, waist-high, and stippling the open lots and ragged roadsides with a blue more heavenly than heaven's own for its having been laid over this earthy ground.

The wild life of Boston is kin to its human life and behaves much the same. You can still find a few Indian families, much mixed, on my edge of the city. So in the dry woods of the Stony Brook Reservation in Roxbury you can still see the last lone chinquapin shrub, *Castanea pumila*. The chinquapin passes, but comes the *galinsoga,* an herbaceous tropical weed from Central America, and climbing up Beacon Hill, enters the ancient and honorable back yards of the Adamses and there makes itself at home.

What a topsy-turvy world! The mighty—how they are fallen! The lines of plant migration are usually from east to west, but this galinsoga upstart has deliberately trekked northward, and dispossessing such aristocracy as had hitherto borne the weight of "the First Church, the Boston State House, Beacon Hill, John Hancock and John Adams, Mount Vernon Street and Quincy," sets up a new aristocracy and takes upon itself this elect burden. Surely Boston's is a wildish destiny!

Would any other metropolitan newspaper than the Boston *Herald* print, as the *Herald* did the other day, a column story of the crow that lives in the neighborhood of Copley Square? Of course the *Transcript* would, and make it four columns. But what other metropolis would have a live wild crow cawing from the weather-vane of its First Spiritualist Temple (now a movie theater)? Or a sacred codfish on its acropolis for an ægis, where the original Greeks had Athena? Perhaps these are better called "totems," after the original tribes of Massachusetts Bay, who called such things "wutohtimoin."

I recently lived for nearly three years at 17 Exeter Street, and an old crow would caw me out of bed all winter long. He remembered his country ways and got up with the milkmen. Born, as I was, in the woods, and brought up in the woods, I felt very much in the woods on Exeter Street, one house removed from Commonwealth Avenue, when the raucous, "Caw! Caw! Caw!" in the stilly dawn would wake me with half conscious thoughts of the barn and morning chores.

Last summer a pair of crows built a nest in one of the cottonwood trees on the corner of Dartmouth and Marlboro streets, one block from where I lived those three years. For some reason

their first nest fell down, nest and eggs an awful
ruin in the street below. But upon the founda-
tion of the old nest a new one went up, and a
better one this time. Passers-by beneath the tree
could see the black head and tail of the sitting
bird. Processions of automobiles went to and
fro all day and half the night; but the crows knew
the mind of Boston, and brooded on, croaking
softly to each other.

"The plowmen homeward plod their weary way."

But they no longer plant corn on the pavements
here. Other carking cares are theirs. And the
crows are returning to hunt for fresh-hatched
sparrows behind the shutters and among the ivied
walls of Commonwealth Avenue!

It is more than a surprising thing to see this
big, black, wary bird back with its nest in the
streets of Boston. What does his presence in the
city portend? He is a hostage, if we will so
accept him. Else he is a spy, an "observer" of
an alien, enemy, power, camped about and investing Boston, the same power that invested Baby-
lon and gave her back to the corbies, temple and
market and court.

"As I was walking all alane,"

(for so the departed spirits do, among their ancient haunts) and found myself at the corner of Commonwealth and Exeter, looking for Number 17,

> "I heard twa corbies making a mane:
> The tane unto the tither did say,
> 'Whar sall we gang and dine the day?' "

And as they flew over me toward a crumbling esplanade of what in my day had been the Charles River, I heard them croaking evenly:

> "Ye'll sit on his white hause-bane,
> And I'll pick out his bonny blue e'en:
> Wi' a lock o' his gowden hair
> We'll theek our nest when it grows bare.

> "Mony a one for him maks mane,
> But nane sall ken whar he is gane:
> O'er his white banes, when they are bare,
> The wind sall blaw for evermair."

This is a melancholy dream. That the Charles may sometime flow past the fallen walls of Boston is wholly possible. But Boston has left a channel for the river, and built a tower for the duck-hawk, and planted cottonwoods for the crows. It is a wise mayor who gives the keys of his city to the crow.

CHAPTER FIVE: A COMEDIAN FROM THE WILD

T̲H̲E̲ March flood was over. The runaway water had crept back into the narrow river-bed, and the wood-choppers were now returned to the timber in order to finish their work. Only a few old trees remained to be felled. Among them, the largest, and perhaps the oldest tree in the timber, was a hollow sycamore that stood high above the banks of the flooded Sangamon, in eastern Illinois. This was a "coon tree." And an old mother coon with a family of six new-born babes was asleep inside at the first fall of the ax.

But she was startled instantly wide-awake. What was it—that tremor? She had never felt a shiver like that before. Then she curled down and cuddled close about the babes. Had she not herself been born in this very tree? It had been a coon tree for generations. Nothing could harm her family here. Yet there it was again—and regularly now, as blow after blow, in ominous succession, sent the dreadful shiver thrilling through the leaning walls and out to every stubby twig high in the air.

This was not the wind. The old coon had weathered many a winter storm in this snug harbor. High in her lofty cabin she had heard the creak of the planking, the twisting and straining of her ship as it rode out the gale. But this was different, as when a ship grounds upon a reef, shuddering from stem to stern.

She saw the light of day in the open doorway overhead. She could escape along the extending limbs. A wild dash—but the babes sleeping in her fur! Then, suddenly, the very universe seemed to stand a moment in breathless terror—poised an instant, stricken, dazed, and undone—when, a mad shriek of winds, a stunning crash, and—all was dust and darkness in the splintered house where a little blind coon was whimpering.

I have dropped into story here in order to vivify the passage of this one wild creature from the timber into human hands. It is a picture of the violence altogether common in our relations with nature. It is a background, also, for a great forgetting and a great accepting on the part of this wild creature after its adoption into a human home.

Wild animals in captivity often change their faces, assuming masks behind which the real creature hides. On the other hand, so-called captivity is often a larger liberty than the wilds allowed, wherein the animal may drop a mask, because it has dropped its wild fears and may behave with a spontaneity and an abandon more revealing of its inner nature than it is ever caught showing in the wilds, or perhaps ever dares to show. It was so with this coon from the sycamore, along the Sangamon in Illinois, and with many another animal I have known.

Nothing is more amazing in the mind of wild life than the quickness with which the most suspicious animal forgets his fears and falls in with human ways. I have seen a tame coyote, and I know nothing more wretchedly abject with fear than a coyote. The miserable creature will shake in an ague of fear at your approach to its cage, though a thousand have passed before you and lifted no hand to harm. But even this sneaking, slinking incarnation of craft and fear has a period of innocency, and if taken young enough, grows up with confidence in man. It is in this frame that some of our wild animals are best studied, for it is in these unmindful moods that the natural creature is most revealing.

The cause of this forgetting of fears and wraths is nothing but the touch of love. In the Field Museum of Chicago are two mounted man-eating lions with a known record for killings unspeakably terrible. As we stand close to the awful muzzles, heavy with underslung jaws, and look into the forward-thrust faces, we sicken at the craft, the strength, the feel of the hot breath upon their victims, and turn away in horror at the thought of the early struggle of human with brute in the bare fight to survive.

The human has won by superior craft over claw and fang, and not only holds dominion, but relentlessly presses forward toward the extinction of his unequal foes, still possessed of his primal fears, still ruled by his ancient wraths, as if he had not discovered that the force which rules all flesh and holds dominion over all worlds is love.

We have not dared to try it on the lion, nor on our neighbor, either. I have seen it work with dogs and horses and bears, and here with this coon from the Sangamon, with the birds in Santa Barbara, and with many a wild thing in Boston.

> He *ruleth* best who loveth best
> All things both great and small;

For the dear God who loveth us,
He made and loveth all,

the poet might have written.

When the great sycamore along the Sangamon
fell, the choppers, hearing a tiny whimpering inside, split the trunk open and found the dead
mother coon and the six little ones. All of these
were alive, but only one of them survived the
shock. This one was not hurt, and took to cow's
milk readily, and was soon holding the bottle himself, for all the world like my little two-year-old
nephew.

Let that boy spy his mother coming with the
bottle, and over he flops on the floor, right where
he is, and, flat on his back, goes at it, legs
sprawled out, fists on the bottle, eyes roving the
whole room, missing nothing, yet betraying nothing of all the many things they see.

This little boy's eyes are blue, but the coon's
eyes were inscrutably black—with mystery and
with tragedy; while all the rest of him seemed
pure comedy. He was a big sham, a bluffer, a
make-believe. He swaggered about, a chip on his
shoulder, hat on the side of his head, coat collar
turned up, college-man style, looking for a real
man's-size job, but finding mostly trouble. A

ladybird, a spool of sewing silk were about his measure.

He had a man's-size growl, though. Indeed, he growled like a bear, like the little bear and the middle-sized bear and the big bear in one great growl! All this was cant and pretense, too. Yet he was no coward. Nothing in the timber, for his size, fights with the skill and courage of the coon. Quick, determined, powerful, and armed with ugly teeth, the coon is a dangerous foe for a dog of twice his weight.

It was his false growl and swashbuckler way which brought the coon of this story to an untimely end. He developed a peculiar fondness for running his fingers through your hair. And all the while he combed, working his forepaws like a shampooing barber into your tousled head, he growled. And he would crouch, and growl, and rush at you, when he came to shampoo, as if he intended to scalp you, falling gently into your hair and closing his eyes as your locks streamed through his funny black paws, the deep growl as sure a sign of comfort and contentment as is the quiet purring of a cat before the fire.

One day he wandered across the fields to the cabin of a neighbor who, tradition said, had never

in all his life been washed or combed. The old
man was asleep on his stoop, his long hair and
bushy whiskers the chance of a lifetime for the
coon. And *Lotor,* "the washer," for that is the
coon's name, was not waiting for an invitation.
Yet he must go through certain motions—crouch-
ing, scratching with his nails, growling, and the
big rush—landing with all-fours in the middle of
Old Lige's Nazarite nest. You can guess what
happened. Old Lige, the heretofore uncombed,
hearing the growling in his sleep, dreamed a
catamount was after him, and when the coon
landed in his hair leaped to his feet, and, snatching a chair on the stoop, struck the "varmint"
dead. The Lodge boys, whose pet the coon was,
wished many a time that their coon had been a
catamount. Old Lige deserved to lose a few of
his whiskers.

The most interesting trait to come to light in
the human freedom allowed this particular coon
was his love of music. No one can watch the
movements of a coon, especially as he walks,
without noting his swaying, rhythmic gait. It is
as if he moved to music. But the coon of the
Sangamon seemed to be gifted, a kind of musical
genius. He was music from his black plantigrade

foot-soles on into the depths of his other soul, if a mere coon has that other soul—as he certainly deserves to have. His walk was rhythm. He did all things to the time of some inner harmony.

The coon had pretty much the run of the house, and when anyone started to play the piano he would come to the door and look in. Allowed to enter, he would respond to the music, if slow and stately, by gravely turning somersaults from the door in a complete circle around the room. No one had taught him to do this. It was his invention, a curious trick of his own, his dance, his cake-walk, which, I suspect, may be something of a custom among his people, could we listen by wireless, and watch by wireless, the secret doings of the wild timber folk, whose lives, more than we yet understand, may move to the music of the spheres.

If the air was lively, the coon would quicken his footing to keep time, turning his somersaults and interspersing them with a kind of Lord Dundreary hop-and-skip—a coon-trot, which was probably the original fox-trot, the human dancers getting their animals mixed. Once around the room, the coon was done and ready to leave the house. He would never respond to an encore.

Later in the summer of that first year of the coon's life, the boys of the household built an outdoor dance floor. The platform was erected in the yard under a large, spreading maple, which was one of the coon's favorite quarters.

On the evening of the first neighborhood dance, the coon was discovered overhead, fast asleep in the crotch of the big maple tree. The young people woke him up, but they could not induce him to come down. The music started. The turning couples began to pour around the platform beneath the now watching coon. Round and round wove the mazy figures to the swinging, swaying rhythms of the waltz, as on and on flowed the bewitching measures of the violins to the tune of

> Treat my daughter kindly,
> And say you'll do no harm;
> And when I die I'll will to you
> My little stock and farm,

the coon overhead slowly coming from his crotch, his paws spread against the bark of the tree, as if invisible forces were hauling at him.

The orchestra stopped amid the clapping of hands, laughter, and dissolving couples, when into the cleared middle of the stage dropped the coon. The musicians were quick with their cue. Catching the very tail of their last tune, they swung on

With all the little chickens in the garden

as the coon, now given the whole stage, took a few fancy steps by way of a flourish, put down his head between his forepaws, and did the aboriginal somersault, over and over, somersault after somersault, around the boards, prancing now a few steps for variation, now with his ringed tail giving a touch of fine fandango, only to stand on his head again, and continue to tumble once all the way around. Then, the music still searching his soul, he marched solemnly off the platform and disappeared into the night.

Nor did he return that night. But the next night when the dance was on, on came the coon for his lone performance, without invitation or partner, for no amount of urging ever prevailed upon him to appear. Just once around, and he would melt away into the moonlight or vanish into the dark.

Deep down in his wild heart was the instinct for play, deep down in all wild hearts, as it lies in all human hearts. What else can the perfect and abounding life of wild animals mean? In the "timber" along the Sangamon in Piatt County that instinct for expression had been repressed since long before the sycamore and the walnut and the redbud were saplings there. But growing up in a human household, free from all natural enemies and restraints, the wild coon forgot that he must wear his finger on his lips, and so gave himself to fun and mischief with all the abandon that human children and puppies and kittens do.

CHAPTER SIX: THE BIRDS OF SANTA BARBARA

THE "high fog" never lifted from the Santa
Ynez peaks all day. Halfway down the
gray-green slopes it hung, and spreading away
to the sea, rolled a billowy, smoky roof above us.
Through the ceiling into our low-posted room an
occasional buzzard would drop out of an upper,
unseen world of wings. It was wings that we
were after, into this foggy world of the buzzard
that we were going, though we knew from the
start that this would be a poor day for birds, and
no day at all for those of the higher altitudes—
the swifts and hawks and eagles. But a day in
the hand, for a bird man, is a day in the bush,
and a burning bush for him, no matter how thick
and wet the weather.

From six in the half-dawn to six in the dull,
chill twilight we searched for wings. I know how
bird-hunterish it sounds to say that, between
dawn and dusk of this unpropitious day, we
identified one hundred and nine species of wild
birds in the field. This is not a record for Santa

Barbara, but it is for me. Two days after our
trip the Commander was again in the field and
brought back one hundred and eighteen species.
I am not boasting. Within the borders of New
York City recently a list of sixty-seven wild
birds was made in a single day, a more significant
census, it seems to me, than ours for Santa Barbara. Ours is nothing sensational. Yet it is
something, something hard to believe, that we still
share the world with so much wild life, that in the
round of a single day anywhere in the United
States we can hear the songs, or see the forms
and colors, and feel the beauty of more than a
hundred species of unmolested native birds.

They ranged all the way from the big, brown
pelican humped in the edge of the surf, to the
jeweled rufous hummer poised before a radiant
passion-flower in a city garden. Santa Barbara
is blessed with birds. Any spot is if it have so
much as a crow.

Four and a half miles from low-water mark
and a bird lights on the rocky crest of the Santa
Ynez range. Shore and sierra, ocean and planted
valley, crowd around Santa Barbara. Where is
there a country of orchards and gardens (and oil
wells) so compacted together, in the midst of

closer embracing mountains and closer girdling
sea? It is a new Hesperides. Over the gardens
bend the round, brown knees of the foothills—unless they are in tender green after the rains, or
of burnished gold as they ripen for the harvest.
Over the foothills rise the walls of the mountains, deep cut with canyons, and deeper cleft
with shadows, green or gray according to season,
reaching up to point and peak, peak linked to
peak in a swinging chain around the sky. And
behind them looms range back of range. And
beyond them other ranges tossed into turbulent
stone, interminable, titanic, the eagle's, and the
condor's unapproachable home.

But we did not so much as look upon much of
this, partly because it was blanketed in fog, and
partly because the dirt roads were quarantined
against the hoof-and-mouth disease, greatly inter-
fering with our movements. As it was we ranged
the beach down to the curving shore of the Rin-
con, then through the great, gray walnut groves
of Carpinteria, thence over the old trail till
stopped by the quarantine officers a little short of
Casitas Pass. Here we turned back by way of the
lemon orchards and the gorgeous gardens of
Montecito, up the Mountain Drive, and down to

the Old Mission—some seventy-three magic miles in all; and one hundred and nine species of birds (not counting the English sparrow) as one way of measuring them.

We named our birds without a gun, "taking" each in its own landscape—birds from the islands offshore, birds of the open fields, birds out of the deep woods, and in from the desert, and down from the highest timber line.

What a spell the single road-runner, the chaparral cock, laid upon the day! It was a glimpse of the Mojave—the cactus, the grease wood, the yucca, and the tinted sands. And the birds from the Channel Islands where the black swift builds, twenty miles at sea! Few ships seem to use the channel, few sails of skiff and sharpie stand against the hazy island walls, where only the fogs and now and then a freighter, and scattering deep-sea fisher craft come and go. Yours are the misty waters, the peaked-propped sky, the mysterious islands, and the kelpy, curving shore. And more truly, humanly yours the close, flanking Sierras.

As the Commander and I wound down the hill from Casa Loma in the dawn and skirted Laguna Blanca, the only fresh-water pond in all the region, we saw hundreds of coot, their white bills gleaming in the thin fog as the plumbeous birds, in widow's weeds, floated quietly under the tules near the shore. With them were canvas-backs, scaups, and one buffle-head, the iridescent purples and greens of his plumage lost in the diffused light of the early day. Out on the turf of the golf course stood a statuesque blue heron, and as we were leaving the pond a bunch of shovelers rounded a point, feeding close together in a little bight among the reeds.

Skirting the town, the Commander turned the car toward the beach. No one of the city was out on the wide sands yet, no one but the birds. They were here, a mixed flock of western and California gulls, wrangling over their breakfast, a few Farallon cormorants on the rail of the pier a silent party to the squabble. Farther out on the rail sat a squat pelican, a mere blur of a bird, still asleep in the fog. We were looking for snowy plovers.

Early the week before I had spent the entire night farther down the beach, tramping the sands till the tide was full, then waking and dozing till the stars began to dim, listening for the cries of these little birds. But I heard only the crash of the surf and the wash of the waves down the shore. I had come particularly for these small plovers, exquisite creatures and unknown to me, and this stretch of beach was their favorite breeding-ground. But though I searched the tiny dunes I found only the sand verbena and the primrose—only a wash of Tyrian purple and old gold over the softly mounded shore.

I had tried too hard. The wee plovers were up at the foot of State Street on the trampled beach waiting for me in the town. We nearly stepped on them. Here they stood fronting us, baby-like birds, their stainless bosoms without an emotion, as quiet as if their hearts were as pure and cold as their snowy breasts. One of them pattered down a wheel rut in the packed sand, stopped and peeked at us, his innocent black eyes, the black bar across his forehead, and the gray crown, looking like some dear child hiding from you behind his chubby hands.

We were now fairly started—and with a flock of snowy plovers! The Commander was to enter this day in red. He keeps a daily record of the movements of the birds, black ink for ordinary days, but red ink for days of ninety species or more. There was a distinct wash of red to things,

I thought; a streak of red across the sea, and something warm—a flush, a reflection of pink, at least, on the all-enveloping fog.

We spoke little, the Commander at the wheel as if he were steering his ship at sea. It was his watch. We understood each other. The Commander did say he wished he had four eyes. I would be content with one bird-eye like the Commander's, his long life at sea, and his years of devotion to the birds East and West, having given him the vision of a hawk. To retire an occasional bird-man like the Commander is a new and worthy use for the navy.

The region about Santa Barbara is a natural bird refuge, and the spirit of the people has made it a sanctuary. Here the land and water birds both find an ideal winter home, the sea and the shore combining in an original A.O.U.—"a more perfect" American Ornithologist's Union than any other I know under the Constitution. The sea-bird rookeries across the channel, the breeding grounds off the coast of Oregon, and the great inland reservations, like the Malhuer in Harney Valley, Oregon, all send their flocks southward in the winter by way of Santa Barbara, and many of the migrants find this as far south as they need to go.

The shore lacks bays and marshes and is woefully wanting in fresh-water lakes and meadows. There is more good bird country on the two shores of Cape Cod than in all the thousand miles of California's coast line. But Cape Cod's winters are horrid at times. From November to April, when the shore birds need hospitality most, it is most denied them, the Atlantic a grudging, churlish host. How gracious the ways of the Pacific by contrast! In the two winters of my sojourn no storm has broken on the Santa Barbara shore, as gale after gale has piled the Chatham bars with wrack, and swept landward with a fury no hand or wing could stay.

Leaving the snowy plovers, the Commander and I soon picked up a pair of surf-ducks, some Hudsonian curlews, and over in the Old Estero, an ill-drained bog in the city not far from the shore, a mated pair of green-winged teal, a cinnamon teal, a sora rail, Forster's terns and tule wrens—words which should be written as music or done with a brush in color.

Or else, possibly, this day's list should have been started in scientific, A. O. U. fashion, with No. 1, the Western Grebe, and closed with No. 767, the Western Bluebird, both of which birds we found. But those are book numbers, the order of the "check-list," and not the order of the open field. Our first bird, waking the Commander at 3 A.M. for our engagement at six o'clock sharp, was the barn owl (No. 365 by the check-list); and the last bird we heard was No. 703a, the Western Mocking Bird, so does the order of life differ from the order of print.

It is interesting that we happened to see A. O. U. No. 1, the Western Grebe; No. 3, the Horned Grebe; No. 4, the Eared Grebe; and No. 6, the Piedbilled Grebe. We also saw No. 10, the Pacific Loon. Then we skipped to No. 44, the Glaucous-winged Gull, a lovely specimen of which we found in an immense flock made up of Western herring, California, ringed-billed, Heermann and Bonaparte gulls.

In this single day we either saw or heard one out of eleven, counting all of the subspecies, of the complete check-list of the United States birds, including the first and next to the last of the full numbers, the smallest of the hummers and the great pelican. If only we had seen the condor, the largest bird that flies! And we might, except for the fog. But the condor's is now a lonely land, and very far away.

One of the thrilling sights to me was a pair of
Brandt's cormorants in wedding dress, the long
filaments on the neck showing beautifully as the
birds came to the surface of the sea below us.
One of them rose, lifting a flapping fish as large
as an alewife, and was instantly attacked by a
Western gull. As the highwayman struck the
water, his wings still unfurled, there was neither
fish nor cormorant in sight, nothing but the wide
unruffled sea. When the cormorant reappeared
a moment later, some dozen yards away, a mere
fish tail wigwagged to the bandit gull.

Most of the birds were in their spring plumage. It was a gallant show! Even the black-
bellied plovers, who must travel slowly up to the
Arctic Circle, had in some individuals put on their
nuptial dress, though several on the beach showed
the mottled transition stage, while others were
wholly white below, as if their natures were
slower and still suspended in a sort of migratory
sleep, unless they were the young of last season.
But how little their wings had slept! From the
polar north down into Brazil, and back to Santa
Barbara since nesting time!

But what were the black-bellied plovers compared, for striking dress, with the black-necked

stilts? The extremes of black and white are not uncommon in nature, and are always a strong combination, but never have I seen these antithetical colors so dazzlingly set over against each other as that day in a group of stilts.

Something must be allowed for my excitement, having never seen the birds alive before, and something also for the dozen of them together, disposed in the grass of the slue less than ten paces from me, and in a manner as if arranged by some artist hand. Jet black they were, from crown to tail above, and snow white below, the two colors, wet from the brush, dividing the birds lengthwise as colors at the water line divide a ship's hull. Here they stood, high on their pink splint legs, suddenly stiff against the green in a dozen poses, staring at me while I stared at them till the dozen ran together as a blur of black and white.

On the beach later I watched one feed and play alone, and in spite of his absurd legs I must say he was a graceful and a most original dancer. It was a cake-walk and more.

For richness and range of color—eight species of wild ducks, all mated or mating, swam into our ken that day! My eye still reels from that cup of color. American mergansers, green-winged and cinnamon teals, shovelers, pintails, canvas-backs, lesser scaups, and ruddy ducks in one framed picture! The East has its share of wild ducks, but where, in one spot, was I ever in the midst of so many kinds before? And all in wedding dress! No painter could put this harlequin flock into a proper frame, perhaps, though nature had. Yet I wish it were on my wall just as I remember it, done in all its iridescence, all of the birds rising long-necked out of the salt hole, the brown of the marsh behind them, in front the surface of the water churned white with the running of the last drake, a gorgeous shoveler showing all his glinting greens and blues and blacks and whites—his chestnut belly, white wing-bars, black bill, and orange feet!

It was still early morning when we reached the Carpinteria Slue and stood looking over the soft green-browns of the marsh, browns of thin sedges and samphire which seemed to wash the feet of the hills. The purple-and gold-laced dunes were immediately underfoot. Cutting through the gently heaving sand poured the shallow slue with the ebbing tide, and on the farther bank, well out in the marsh, erect and watchful, the center of the picture, stood a white egret, his bent shoulders piled with overlapping plumes as pure as spun snow. Flanking him, their heads high and motionless, a tall blue heron and a brown bittern waited to see us pass, while volleying up the twistings of the slue whirled a cloud of Western sandpipers—like rain, like snow, as back or belly up they wheeled and banked upon the muddy shallows. And overhead, with muffled honk, three lesser snow geese, misty figures, steering northward through the fog!

Taking care to spare the inlay of flowers over the tiny dunes, we turned in our tracks to face a world of shore and surf where the long-billed curlews were probing, and a pack of little sanderlings were pattering at the heels of the receding waves. Back they scamper as the new breaker combs over and reaches for them with spread, sudsy fingers far up the sands. On the side where the slue makes into the ocean I counted eleven pelicans in conclave, with gulls and terns, and a few spotted sandpipers resting near them. Offshore, over the slowly heaving lines of kelp, were some hundreds of cormorants, dark stormy figures, stretched in long undulating strings, one bird exactly behind the other, and all so close to the surface as scarcely to clear the water, more reptilian than bird-like, as if monster winged serpents were crawling swiftly on the sea.

Yet so near are the mountains landward, and nearer still the bean fields, the walnut groves, and the gardens, that we saw a California yellow warbler on the kelpy rocks, a Western kingbird hawking over the shore, and here with the sea fowl, where land and channel meet, the red-shafted flicker, the flat-headed jay and the mourning dove. Neighbors to an ancient cypress, which leans hard from the bluff above the beach, are some scraggly tobacco trees. The ancient cypress is a well-known cormorant roost. The tobacco trees blow their golden trumpets for the humming birds, Anna, and rufous, and the black-chinned, who dart and squeak and fight among the blossoms that are wet by the salty spray.

Born a woodsman, not a sailor, I grew up, however, with sailors, and have always had a ship of my own at sea. To this day the shore birds stir me strangely; and the pounding of the surf, which I could faintly hear at night from Casa Loma, forever calls me, a Viking voice out of a far ancestral past. But I have been long ashore and deep in the woods. And when the Commander turned our craft toward the hills I was quite ready to drive.

California is not a warbler country. It lacks the deep woods which the warblers love. The chaparral-covered Sierras and the sage- and cactus-grown deserts are not for them. Among the live oaks and sycamores of the dry streams, and especially among the willows along the trickling Casitas Creek, we found a few warblers, the lutescent, Audubon, black-throated gray, California yellow, Macgillivray, and golden pileolated, and hiding deep in the tules of the Old Estero, the western yellow-throat—a fair showing for California. Any migration day in Massachusetts could make a better showing.

I shall not catalogue my ships, though I know well the interest for bird-lovers of such a field list. Grant me the joy of naming the finches, please—willow, and green-backed, Cassin, California, purple, and the common house finch; and with them the sparrows—Belding, Nuttall, golden-crowned, chipping, and San Diego song sparrows; and with them the bush-tit, wren-tit and titmouse, just to stir a bit of jealousy in certain hearts I know!

If I turn reporter here it is because there is no other way to suggest the variety and beauty of the bird life which still survives the unthinkable warfare we have waged so long against it. Only those who know the birds can understand all it means to find, in the course of a single day, the Arizona hooded oriole, the black-headed grosbeak, the lazuli bunting—a fairy bird—and Hutton's vireo, all of them new to the observer! To the uninitiated these names mean little, but for those who can translate them in terms of shape and song and color there must be weeping at the thought of what they missed on April 8 about Santa Barbara.

As good as the birds was the Commander. He was not altogether a new species to me, though I had never known his like to be retired from the navy. Yet you find a few of them scattered the world around. We have one in Hingham, though he is not retired. He knows the plants. There is nothing of the plant kind in Massachusetts whose whole life story he cannot tell. And he has hay fever at that! To tramp afield with him is to find that your old familiar fields are the Elysian Fields. And so with the Commander. And who is better fit to tramp the fields with bird-glasses after his years of standing watch at sea?

On our way along the Foothill Drive we were rounding a sharp turn in the road when a chaparral cock glided across our bows, a swift, shadowy thing. The next instant, as if the two might have been watching each other, a coyote crossed the other way in front of us, so like the road-runner as for a second to make me think the bird had doubled and recrossed with lightning speed.

So furtively did they fade into the brush that, had the day brought us nothing more, it had been a notable day for me. Just the glimpse of this long, streaked shape, this erect bronzy crest, this disproportionate tail, and this uncanny four-footed gait of the road-runner would have made it a day for me to enter in red. This mere flash of the bird was a contact with a feathered personality so strikingly eccentric as to be unforgettable. The creature seems more like something in scales, and not quite belonging to human times.

The road-runner is, indeed, a denizen of arid and humanly uninhabitable places, a spirit of the desert, and best fits the extreme and distorted landscape there. He has come out among men, as men have gone into the deserts to him. A pair of the strange creatures build in the dense thickets about Casa Loma, just as a pair of coyotes den in the hillside close to the house, showing nothing but amity and a sincere effort to dwell together in peace with their human neighbors.

But the stage for the road-runner's true rôle must be set in the desert, against the sand and sage, when the mesquite and the cactus are in bloom, and when the bird can be seen feeding upon scorpions, centipedes, lizards, and horned toads. Strong meat this. But the road-runner is a strong character. I chased one with an automobile and found he was doing better than twenty miles to the hour, doing it easily, and carrying the while in his beak the desiccated body of a sparrow hawk.

It was along the Foothill Drive that I picked up the mangled body of a black-headed grosbeak, the first I had ever held in my hand. It may have flown against the telephone wires; but the chances are that some orchardist had shot it for destroying fruit. I took up the blot of colors, beautiful in their confusion, the black and white and cinnamon, and the bright yellow under-wing coverts, like a smeared fragment of some painter's palette.

As day declined the Commander brought me back to town on a very special errand up the mountain road above the Mission. He wished to show me two rare birds, the sure reward for our long day in the field. He knew exactly where to go, even to a particular bend in the road for one bird, and to a certain bowlder a mile farther on for the other. For years the Commander had been taking his elect friends up to this turn, where you get the first look far out over the city, to see, not the city, no, no, but the little rufous-crowned sparrow.

We had already seen the golden-crowned sparrow; but that was not this bird. Far from it. Let the wise smile over this difference in crowns. These things are hidden from the wise and prudent, and revealed only to the simple and the pure in heart, like the Commander.

We drew up on the edge of the steep turn, watched and waited, beat about the rocks, up and down the slope, but no rufous-crowned sparrow appeared. This is the only spot in all the region, so far as anybody knows, where this small bird can be seen. And the Commander had never

failed to find him here. But he failed this time.
What of it! And I began to count up for him
the new birds which the day had brought. He
was not to be consoled. Had he not kept this
bird to the last, this and one other? Anybody
might easily have seen all that we had to-day.
Only the Commander could show me the rufous-
crowned sparrow. It was always here! But not
to-night. Besides it was rapidly growing dark
and there was yet the rock wren to show me, almost as rare a bird about Santa Barbara as the
rufous-crowned sparrow, and much more of a
character.

We cruised on up the heights and down to the
reservoir, beyond which lay a rocky pasture.
The Commander was now lying forward on the
lookout, his arms completely encircling the steering wheel, his gaze bent across the dusky field.
We had tarried overlong. This rock wren had
been promised me for many days, ever since the
Commander had made up his mind that I was
one who would understand.

The rock wren is a very interesting bird, not
at all wrenlike in shape or habit, though, like the
family, eccentric and individual in its ways. In
its altitudinal nesting range it probably sur-

passes any other known bird, being found in Death Valley below sea level, on the Farallone Islands off San Francisco Bay, and in the high Sierras, up, at least, as far as 12,500 feet. From the humid sea coast and the hottest desert up above the timber line among the coldest peaks he ranges, nesting and at home! About Santa Barbara he nests in crevices of rocks, or under the bowlders in open spaces, and is said to lay a tiny pavement of pebbles for several inches up to his nest.

The Commander was anxious to show the bird to me, the closing feature, the climax of our day. But it was now very chill and late. The shadows creeping far down the canyons were about to stop our hunting.

We rounded a promontory in the road and the Commander throttled down. His bird-hunting craft was beautifully trained. It seemed to know where the birds were, so long had it hunted them, so many had it found. It came creeping up the ridge, chugging softly, looking with headlights and radiator for the little wren, the Commander looking, too, as if every bowlder were an iceberg and this the Northwest Passage over the top of the world.

Then we stopped. And there on the top of a piece of granite which lay in the shadow of a great bowlder, stood a tiny gray bird, bobbing, bowing, making no sound, but saying a great deal. Its head was drawn down between its shoulders, weariness written all over its being, as, curtsying like a tired child, it plainly whimpered: "I told you I would wait. But I can't do it another minute. I'm sleepy and cold. I've been bobbing here in the fog all day long, right here on the top of this stone; but you didn't come."

This is what the Commander heard him say, even if I didn't. And he whispered excitedly to me: "You go round by the prow. I'll go aft by the stern. I want you to get a good look at him." We had arrived a little late. The tiny chap with a last quick, but proper curtsy, bobbed from the top of the rock and was gone.

As the Commander came back to the ship and clambered aboard, he pulled out his log-book and wrote, "108, the Rock Wren." But it might have been, judging by the quiver about his silent lips: "We have met the enemy and he is ours." As for me, I was saying over to myself with more wonder and understanding than ever before:

As for the stork
The fir trees are her house,
The high hills are a refuge for the wild goats,
And the rocks for the conies.

This was the country of the burrowing owl, and this was his hunting hour; but though we swung slowly through the dusking pastures we neither saw nor heard him. It looked as if our day's hunt were done. Descending, we hurried back to the Old Mission for a chance sight of the cliff swallows which nest under the covings of that ancient structure. It was cold by this time, and the fog and the early spring twilight must certainly have put an end to all insect flight and all hawking by the swallows. But we were not sure that the birds had returned from the south.

We turned in behind the garden of the Mission and searched the roofs and coves in the failing light. There was not the flutter of a wing or a single twitter. Not back yet, and our day was done.

Then I heard the Commander mutter something, or try to. He was gazing up into the sky. And there under the floor of the fog and gloom sailed a cloud of new birds, not cliff swallows,

but Western martins, more martins than either
of us had ever seen in a flock before.

Did that cloud cover and transfigure me as it
did the Commander, the Mission garden, the
towers and bells and the city lying below and the
distant sea? If not transfigured, I was instantly
transported—to early childhood and the old
home dooryard and the purple martins about the
barn! They were my first birds. A double row
of martin houses extended across the whole back
end of that big barn, the colony inhabiting them,
to my childish fancy, thousands and thousands
strong.

It was nearly six o'clock when we left the
Mission. With the exception of the barn owl in
the early morning, and the screech owl which the
Commander added at seven that night, we had
made our list since six in the morning, not an un-
important bag for an ornithologist, but a much
more important bag for a human being. It is a
difficult thing to make clear to the uninitiated,
but the Commander and I know.

We might have found a larger number, as the
Commander did two days later. We might yet
pick up a night bird on our way home. But we
rounded Laguna Blanca with nothing more,

hearing only the quiet talk of the coots on the water and the calling of a wild drake. The night before a great horned owl had been hooting in the live oaks about Casa Loma. Only the fog blew in now, weaving like a wraith among the stooping trees.

It was something short of midnight when a mocking bird broke into song outside my window. He was already counted in the list. A slow breeze laden with the bloom-piled boughs of the acacia trees stepped into the room from the garden. The bird sang on,

"As if its song could have no ending,"

when suddenly it stopped, and booming thickly through the muffle of the fog came the rounded, "*Woo-ooo, woo-ooo, woo-ooo, woo-oo-oo-ah*" of the great horned owl. "One hundred and ten!" I cried, jumping from my bed. But it was now past midnight, and this was number one on the list of another day.

CHAPTER SEVEN: YELLOW-BILLED MAGPIES

THE spell of weather, a "high fog" for the most part, which for more than a week had begloomed the scenes and souls of Santa Barbara, was now working itself into a real storm, a real California storm, of drifting, driving sand instead of bourgeoning rain.

"A great movement in real estate," remarked the Commander, dryly, as we faced the scouring blast. "But we'll run out of it by the time we cross the Pass. It won't bother the magpies, anyway, and it *has* blown off the fog. If we get a clear sky on the other side of the range we ought to do some good work in the upper air."

The words thrilled me. We were out for yellow-billed magpies, rare enough birds for a day of great adventure; but what did "good work in the upper air" mean except eagles, too, and white-throated swifts, and condors, possibly? What a world for the bird-lover was this California country!

I had my private doubts about the magpies,

threatened now too long with extinction. Condors I knew were over the range, but I had never seen one a-wing! Morning after morning when the sky was clear I had searched the Santa Ynez peaks for condors, but nothing larger than a turkey buzzard had sailed over the heights. And now the Commander implied condors, I was very sure. Condors and yellow-billed magpies the same day! Just too much!

So it proved. We saw no condor! Yellow-billed magpies, we did see, though—making the motor trip from Boston to Santa Barbara worth while! We did good work in the upper air, too, watching the nose-dive of a golden eagle from the sky, and the hawking of a colony of white-throated swifts. We did even better than that when we caught the flash of a single black swift, over from the Channel Islands, as he whipped about the shoulder of a mountain not far above our heads. But there is still an unseen condor in my sky, though I know where in Fish Creek Valley to camp for him when I come again to California. I have seen the yellow-billed magpies, and California has few rarer sights to show.

We should have waited for a better day. Coming from Massachusetts, I was not inured to California winters. I even lacked clothes. The Commander was dressed for it, this sort of thing quite to his liking, reminding him of his early days aboard the *Albatross* around the Horn and working with the fur seals up in Bering Sea. There was the touch and tang of spray in the sting of the subcutaneous sand. As for fit days—there is only one, and we were taking it.

This species of storm was as new to me as the birds we were hunting, an earthy thing with wings, all grit to the teeth, gravel to ears and eyes, a builder of dunes on the road in front of our car, dissolver of the stable hills, sifting a new sierra from the sky. We should have chosen to-morrow, the perfect day. All the great things that never happen come off to-morrow. The sky will be full of condors to-morrow. But the Commander said we might get a little closer, possibly, to the magpies on account of the heavy wind. And there might be no sand on the other side of the Pass.

So it turned out. The wind continued unabated, but the upper air about the crags of the Pass was clear, and on this other side of the range we found entirely different weather—and a new bird to me.

It would be untrue to say that I had motored across the continent (4,040 miles by my speedometer) to see a yellow-billed magpie. I'm nearly fool enough for that, and the Commander is more of a bird man than I am. He is a yellow-billed crank, and a resident of Santa Barbara where the type specimen of the yellow-billed magpie was taken by Nuttall, and in honor of him named *Pica Nuttalli*. The bird has never been found outside of the narrow limits between Santa Barbara and the San Joaquin Valley, and not since Nuttall's day has a specimen been taken within fifty miles of Santa Barbara.

But the Commander would take me to them, about fifty miles away. Having heard nothing of them since Bradford Torrey's story some dozen years before, I feared the birds might have vanished. No, no. The Commander knew a clump of willows in a little barranca over Gaviota Pass (the "Pass of the Gull") where he was sure to see them—six of them. And another colony of seven at the foot of the Pass, and eleven miles farther on a colony of two.

We descended the Pass to the first ranch house and searched the sycamores in vain for the seven birds. Just as I knew it would be. The Commander would lead one to think these birds were stuffed and permanently mounted on their colony trees. I did not know the Commander so well then as I do now.

How could it be otherwise with birds so few and sought for? I had seen the Torrey pine farther down the California coast, a tree more locally distributed even than this magpie bird, and having an habitation so restricted, so confined and hazardous, that its bare existence strikes one almost with terror, by so narrow a margin, by so small a number of specimens, has the ancient creature escaped the hand of Time.

The pine is now in sanctuary; not the bird, though it is just as worth saving. The Torrey pine is herded into a smaller corral than any other tree in the United States. Now if we could give the tree wings, so it could fly, we should have something of the puzzle of the yellow-billed magpies. The seeds of the Torrey pine have wings. They can fly. And why they have not carried their dying race farther afield is hard to say. The case of the magpies is harder still, for birds belong to a higher order of beings than trees. Birds can be hungry, and frightened, and pursued, not to mention their being curious about the other side of the mountain. But these yellow-billed magpies seem as little traveled, and racially as arrested, as the Torrey pine. And this is their peril, though earlier it may have been their safety. Known now to reside only in certain definite places, and that they are to be found there the year around, how can the bird escape its many enemies? How has it escaped so long? Twenty years before this visit of mine Mrs. Florence Bailey had written of the bird:

In a restricted area in the San Joaquin and Sacramento valleys in California some of the yellow-billed magpies are still left; but they are so much in evidence, and afford such a tempting target, that the days of the little band are probably numbered.

That inevitable fate had overtaken them, I reasoned; these in the colony at the foot of the Pass had been wiped out. And I should find it true of the rest of the species. I had arrived too late.

We moved on past the sycamores to the older, better established colony in the barranca. As we drew up by the side of the road, the great coast road, El Camino, a pair of splendid birds rose from the willows along the nearly dry stream,

swung in a slow easy curve above our heads, and
tobogganed gracefully down to a white oak on
the other side, the sun blazing gloriously upon
their black and white plumage and *golden* bills!

It was a little too theatrical, too well-timed
and automatic! The Commander was making
sport of me, a tenderfoot from Hingham.
Painted birds against a painted barranca! And
when I stared and accused him of "compact" and
of "compositioun," to use the terms of Chaucer,
he ran his tongue around his dry lips as if to utter
something. But it was no occasion for words.

They were real birds—real yellow-billed magpies. And yonder was a third one on the hillside. And here in the willows and oaks above
the little creek were the big roofed nests of the
colony. We counted four different birds all told,
and from their behavior, and from the appear-
ance of the nests, we were pretty sure that other
birds were in the coarse stick houses brooding.

The Commander wet his lips again, a sign, I
came to understand later, of inward and pro-
found satisfaction.

And it was a sight to travel far to see, but not
because of the landscape, for there was nothing
peculiar about that, nor about this particular

spot, except a little water. One could not help but ask, Why are the birds here and not at a hundred places as likely as this along the road? Back a mile or two the Commander assured me was a colony of seven, ahead eleven miles was a colony of two, and nowhere else in the country-side, so far as he knew, a single other yellow-billed magpie.

Nor had these three situations anything in common which marked them for magpies. Willows and oaks and water in one; sycamores and oaks but no water in another; and in the third a few scattered live-oaks on the steep slope of a rocky pasture. All three situations had the common highway, however, the least safe and reasonable feature, one would think, for a village of rare and showy birds.

I asked the Commander to take me to the colony eleven miles ahead. It was an April day. The Commander had not visited that colony since August the summer before, but off he started. I marked the speedometer. At exactly eleven miles ahead we drew up again by the roadside on a curve, a slight thing by which to mark a spot in a road which was a constant curve. But there below us, tossing over the dried chips of cow

manure, looking for insects underneath, was a
magpie with a yellow bill.

This seemed strange indeed. To stop in
August and see this bird, then to drive straight
here in April and find him exactly where he was
last seen, gave me a new glimpse of bird life.
Barnyard fowl must use their wings as much as
these birds, and are not much more confined!

Interesting revelations of the methodical habits of birds, their timed coming and going, and
the amazing accuracy of their sense of direction
on their trails, are just now coming to light
through the work of the bird-banders. The stars
in their courses are hardly more punctual than
the migratory birds in theirs. But what other
bird seems so like a star in its fixed constancy as
this yellow-billed magpie?

We waited by the roadside and watched this
single bird, hoping to see his mate. She may
have been brooding, but neither she nor her nest
was in sight. I could scarcely believe that the
striking creature below us was not tethered or
pinioned. If he could use his black and white
wings, gleaming bronzy blue in the sunshine,
what tied him so to this patch on the hillside?
Every time the sharp gust caught him it filled

his unreefed tail and warped him into the breeze facing us, his golden bill as big as a toucan's to our greedy eyes.

Not rooted like the oaks, yet his homing instinct striking down as deep into the earth, held him like an oak to his place. Here in August, here in April, here the Commander assured me he could be seen every day of the calendar, as if he never moved beyond this bend in the highway, or up over the hill, or down into the bottom of the valley.

A fresher green than old Chaucer sang, because it had followed a longer drought, poured over the slope and spread deep into the winding valley. The live-oaks were in tender leaf and blossom, the little tits already weaving the delicate yellow flowers into their hanging nests. Bending above this green and gold was the blue and gold of the California sky. But what was so pure a gold as the bill of the magpie? All was background and frame for him. Clean cut, elegant, and daringly marked, he wore the air of a prince—or was it the bandmaster? The way he tossed those dried chips over seemed to turn the very manure to music!

One wide, circular disk was too much for him

to tip. He came stiffly up to it, in full evening
dress, inserted his gold bill beneath the edge, and
flung his head carelessly. The flat thing wheeled
half around and flopped back, the bird moving
on before the end of the performance, not giving
so much as a second glance at the thing, subsist-
ence for him being no affair of shirtsleeves.
He was not one to grub for a living—not with his
bill of gold!

So at least the worshipful Commander and I
interpreted it.

Tastes, training, his family's past and its present exclusive position, were clearly manifest to
our excited imaginations in this fine gesture. As
the bird walked away proud, erect, with just a
touch of hauteur in his carriage, I thought I had
never seen anything more self-contained and
aristocratic.

Perhaps his vanishing country and fading
numbers are partly due to something defiant and
unadaptable in his nature. He is without curios-
ity, is completely self-centered, lacking in ordinary interest about people and places evidently,
so lacking as never to travel a mile from home.
As human families of like temper and aloofness
run out from consequent isolation and inbreed-

ing, may it not be so with this ancient family of the yellow-billed magpies?

This is too fanciful. Yet what other bird, with wings, do I know who stays so determinedly in his rooftree or who carries about with him an air of such absolute self-sufficiency? Compare him with the pushing English sparrow or the quail and crow, or that good mixer the robin. By contrast, think of the wandering-tattler that I saw on the Santa Barbara beach a few days since— just arrived from the Galapagos Islands, and on his way to the coasts of Alaska, if report be true, before he settles down to nest for the short summer on the boggy banks of the Yukon! If the wandering-tattler is an infrequent visitor and his family is few, it may be from too much travel, the extreme hazards a-wing for ten months of the year over the wide Pacific altogether more than the hardiest stock can stand.

What in life is so widely variant as our temperamental differences? See in these two birds how that extreme difference expresses itself in mind and body—the tattler semi-webbed of foot, fore-and-aft rigged, loving the surf and forever at sea, the magpie with so much more rudder than sail that he must almost unship his tail before he can take to the air. One who has a tail that stays behind like the yellow-billed magpie's must stay behind with his tail.

Tail or temper (the two are very much the same), it seems almost inexplicable that any flying bird should stay so like a serf to a plot of soil. He moves from one side of the road to the other, from the oaks to the willows. But the trees also wave their arms in the breeze and move almost as far.

Mother Goose, to have her children safe abroad, would keep them safe at home, a practice prevailing among the yellow-billed magpies, but which is by no means reassuring. The yellow-bills are prolific birds, clutches of seven eggs being not uncommon among them. They are good home-builders, too, thatching their rough, strong nests and entering them from beneath the roofs on the sides. They are apparently faithful parents and mates. Yet from season to season there is no increase in numbers among them, but rather a slow falling off. Has the family physically run out? Or has it become imaginatively and socially unfit?

One would like to ask, How came the yellow-billed family here, in this narrow strip between the Sierras and the sea, and nowhere else? And how came their bills to be yellow when all other magpies, a great and flourishing family, have bills that are black?

Some ornithologists believe the California bird of the yellow bill to be the progenitor of the black-billed race, the first one of whom, born with a black bill, a little larger body, and a more adventurous spirit, went eastward over the Sierras, discovering there a larger, more difficult world, and, put to it, conquered the new country and grew with it great as a race and strong. The parent birds with the golden bills stayed where we still find them, root-bound like certain plants, or more like certain residual persons, slowly dwindling to a vanishing point in their outlived land.

Foolish imaginings that leave us with more, instead of with fewer, questions! Why, for instance, holding on as these birds do from decade to decade, cannot they do a little better and go forward even by the narrowest of margins? And why have they not been annihilated long ago?

As I sat watching the few proud birds in the barranca colony I shivered to think how easily a soulless collector could take every one of them,

how with no warden to stay him he could wipe
out in a day of shooting the last bird of this
golden-billed race.

They are enough to tempt any greedy or
thoughtless man with a gun. A thousand automobiles, probably, speed through their rookery
every day. I wish that I could build a wall about
them or lay out a different highway down the
coast, avoiding Gaviota Pass. But none of these
things would stop the desire to kill. Other birds,
less striking to the eye, and more remote than
the yellow-billed magpies, have hurried away
from the gun, never to come back. We must
take away the gun, but better we must take away
the desire to kill, and for guns give eyes, and for
the desire to kill give joy in seeing.

A little smaller than their black-billed cousins,
they differ in the field only in respect to their
yellow bills. Head and breast are black, the jet
swinging in more than half a perfect circle from
shoulder to shoulder against the snow white of
belly and sides. The ten-inch tail with its grad-
uated feathers is black. The wings at rest are
black, but spread, they show that nine primaries
are only edged with black, the rest of the
feather white, the color scheme a kind of picket-

pattern, which seen in flight, balanced by two
half-moons of white upon the bird's back, fairly
dazzle the eye, the whole flourish more like one
of the old Spencerian pen pictures than the
planned shape and arrangement by Nature of a
living form.

The zebra is not more consciously marked,
though he is supposed to be camouflaged for protection, his colors laid on by the old jungle
painter who loved and laughed while he worked.
It was a sign painter who did the magpie, and if
he had plotted the destruction of the bird he
could hardly have made him a more conspicuous
mark. And then his bill of gold!

But California can possibly keep this remain-
ing gold. She once had dust as yellow as this,
which the 'Forty-niner carried away and scattered, leaving her none the poorer, however.
There is small distinction in gold. Arizona and
Nevada mine gold, and all the states make gold,
and pour it back into the lap of California. Gold
is common. But not the gold of California sun-
shine and magpies. Neither Arizona nor Nevada
produces these birds with golden bills, and once
they are scattered they will not come back as
comes the 'Forty-niner's gold. Let these few

birds perish and neither California nor the whole round world shall see them more. But the willows would weep in the little barranca over Gaviota Pass.

What is the glory of California? Not her cities. John Muir's first question on landing in San Francisco was, if tradition be true, "What is the quickest way out of this town?" Los Angeles seems almost as big and terrible as Chicago. Not her big cities, but her big trees—these are her glory, as the Sierras and the desert are her grandeur. These are her ancient past, her present, and her future—these and the Torrey Pines, and the great condors and the handful of magpies with the yellow bills.

The first rush to California was into her ravines for gold. The second rush was into her valleys for orange lands. The third rush was into her deep sands with drill and pump for oil. The gold is gone. The fruit lands are taken. The oil begins to fail. But not the coming of those who would be warmed by the golden sun, and healed by the sovereign air, and fed by the beauty of the Sierras, and freed among the purple spaces of the Mojave from narrow streets and trampling things. These keep coming in ever-increasing numbers—more than the 'Forty-niners, more than the homesteaders, more than the drillers for the oil, seeking a better country for body and soul.

Slow to restore her ancient missions, swift to dig her irrigation ditches, California, like her sister states, only dimly apprehends the spiritual values, that they are the eternal values—the cloudy head of the redwood, not the square feet of lumber in his massive bole. California has a sanctuary for the Torrey Pines. One may not pick up so much as a fallen needle under these bent and weary trees. Unfit for the mill, bowed down and dwarfed by their forgotten years, these pines are pure spirit, and their leaves are for the healing of the nation.

So are the condors and the magpies ministering spirits. Arise, O sun-kissed Sister of the States! Ascend the high places in your Sierras and make every peak a safe perch for the condor. Go over Gaviota Pass and build a sanctuary for the magpies, a holy place of that barranca among whose willows the last of the yellow-billed birds still make their nests.

. . . .

A thousand automobiles pass that barranca

without a stop. But I saw one from Massachusetts draw up by the roadside, and one from New York, and one from Virginia. To-morrow more shall stop and more and more. For if the oil fails the sunshine shall never fail. The earthquake may bring to its knees the proud and foolish city, but never the Sierras slumbering by the sea. I have seen a fire blacken their gray-green flanks, and then the high-fog sweep in and cover them with their chaparral cloaks again. And the Mojave shall burn and blossom with supernal dusks and dawns. And from the level West, and peopled East, from snows and bitter winds, a constant caravan shall come to see the magpies with the golden bills, the seasons with the golden months, the orchards with the golden fruit, the daily miracle of the desert twilight, the hills, the sea, the ancient cypress trees and Torrey Pines. And some of them, standing uncovered where the Big Trees stand, shall be aware of God.

CHAPTER EIGHT: STILL I GO FISHING

I

I DREAM of a day when we shall cease from killing—for business in war, and for sport in the field. Yet still I go fishing. An old weakness of the flesh, that; a "throw-back," as the scientists say, from my savage, ancestral past. I love to fish. I hate to kill. I put a flopping fish to death at once—and almost spoil my outing. But I cannot see the creature gasping in the air. Death that way is too terrible. So I forget—and fish and hanker after every small boy I see with a pole and a can of worms.

Just now I am sitting with a pencil on the porch of our Santa Barbara home watching two men on little Laguna Blanca below me whipping the surface with spoons and spinners. Every time they hit the water there seems to be a splash, a shining leap into the air, and a flapping bass tumbling into the bottom of the boat.

I am trying to stay with my pencil. One should be calm with a pencil. But a flapping fish at the end of any line is not to be written about.

It is to be taken off and a fresh bait put on quickly. I watch the fishermen below me and count!

As a boy I hunted. Every boy in the country parts did when I was a boy. And there was good hunting. I fished when I was a boy, too, and if one keeps on fishing, one will always be a boy. So I fish. No desire is left in me to shoot, to join that army of destruction which civilization has long since discharged, but which, as guerrillas and snipers and pot-hunters must shortly pick off the last wild animal form. The sight of a man with a gun about my fields makes me sick.

The streams and ponds are different. They can so easily be restocked. And the sea, if fished with care, is utterly inexhaustible. Even the fur seal has had his Arctic waters posted to insure his precious pelt. Yesterday the papers told of a mighty herd of whales which had been seen in the north Atlantic, more than had been sighted for many years. And with war prices still prevailing and the cost of food steadily mounting, fresh mackerel are quoted to-day in the Eastern markets at ten cents a pound! I sit here on the porch of Casa Loma and watch the two fishermen on the little artificial lake below me, and I grip my stubby pencil as if it were a maple pole.

Nevertheless, I have cast no hook into Laguna Blanca, partly because it is private water and permission to fish is a matter of friendship and favor, and partly because the water which pours into the pond, when it does pour, pours through an iron pipe and runs out of the pond by "osmosis" up the tall stems of the tules, and by evaporation around the tepid margins of the pool, where the sun tries to cool himself, but drinks and sweats all day long.

I had a mill-pond to fish in when I was a boy, wood-walled, with margins overhung by willow, magnolia, and wild grape vines, whose water was deep and dark and sweet to drink, and cold, coming by a hundred sandy streams through the spicy shadows of an ancient cedar swamp.

There are no such ponds in Santa Barbara. I am sorry for all Santa Barbara boys, who have to stand head-high in a process of osmosis to fish. They fish the breakers along the Santa Barbara beach, however, and that is wild and thrilling. I wonder if there is a truly desolate boy with a hook and line from Boston to Santa Barbara?

Did I say I had *a* mill-pond to fish in when I

was a boy? I had a baker's dozen of them, and a
real river, and a creek, and a big bay, and the sea.
I couldn't escape becoming a fisherman. No boy
can pick his parents or the place in which he
ought to be born. I have thought over that a
great deal, and it may sound queer, but if I could
have chosen, I should have picked the very parents I had and the same unheard-of place where
I was born.

No such landscape lay about me when a child
as stretched below and above me in Santa Barbara; nor could there be any landscape more
varied or quite so lovely anywhere else in the
world.

The sun climbs up the sky over the back of
Casa Loma hill, throwing soft shadows through
the live-oaks down upon the sleeping pond.
Triple tule walls encircle the oval water, green
and brown and mauve, outside of whose deep
ranks a yellow road swings wide around, bor-
dered on the distant side with lines of spreading
palm trees, suggesting heathen in their darkness,
and coral strands, and tropic things all strange
to me.

And billowy and brown behind the arching
palms, billow back of billow, roll the harrowed

bean fields of Hope Ranch, with dark live-oaks about their domes. And back of these brown hills the abrupt Sierras, and back of these, and over all, the blue arched California sky! I cannot close my eyes and dream a scene so fair as this, with here and there a house, a gray-green walnut orchard, the winding of a train between the hills, and westward, where the wooded headland breaks, a vista of the sea.

The little lake, Laguna Blanca, lies just below me through the tree-tops down the sharp hill slope of Casa Loma. I cannot dive into the water from my study window, but I can look into the jeweled pool and even hear the quiet talk of the coot and the ducks and the sandpipers. Every day I sit and watch a group of wild whistling swan who are passing a part of their winter here, visitors from the far north. As this is the only fresh water in the vicinity, except for a small, walled-in reservoir above the town, there is a constant procession of wild bird life coming in from the sea, and over the peaks of the Santa Ynez, and winding down against the background of the mountains to drink and bathe and rest upon the bosom of the pool.

Perhaps the fishers see all this. But they are

very busy in their boat. Besides, the high walls of the tules shut them in, while I am up above them on a mountain of my own, with wings, almost, of my own.

Then evening comes. And when the sun goes down into the sea, or swinging with the season north across the soft brown hills, stands for one glorious moment on the mountain-top, my cup is full. For into my brown earth bowl from out the azure chalice of the sky pours down the lambent light, flooding Laguna Blanca, kindling among the tules into opalescent flames that flash and fade with ashes of quicksilver.

And I'm content with this, with waiting here inside the closing gates, with watching of the swans, the tiny tractors combing over the chocolate hills, the high scarred mountains, the sea, the sky, and these two fishers in their boat. Not, I hope, that I am ill or tired. I will say that I drove my car every mile of the way from Hingham here, which was not the fun of tired men, or men grown very old. Then why am I less for fishing now and more for watching that old blue heron standing on one leg behind the tules thinking?

I have grown wary of my time, perhaps, and

for fear some finny hour from the larger deep
swim past me and escape I do not dare to fish?
I have lost many a precious hour of the hurrying
flood, but never one while fishing. I hooked
them, every one, and landed every hour of them,
a good catch as I count hours now.

But these men on the lake are catching only
fish. If that were fishing, then I should try my
luck on Laguna Blanca, though I never used a
spoon and spinner, nor asked permission of any
person smaller than a state, nor ever cast my
hook into an artificial pool. Under these conditions I might think I was picking apricots on
Laguna Blanca. Fishing has somewhat to do
with fish. It has very much to do with worms
and poles and corks and mill-ponds and persimmon trees. It has nothing to do with permits,
but everything to do with freedom, and being
still like the great blue heron.

That old blue heron and I were taught to fish
in the same school. I think that I can expect
more from beneath a bunch of lily-pads, and wait
longer for it, than he, though I have watched him
stand without a move for nearly half a day. But
he is the true angler, and like all anglers has a
turn for philosophy and is given much to dreams.

What if such dreams when brought to gaff are sculpins! They are fine fish beneath the water, these that bite and get away.

I cannot go a-fishing where there is nothing to catch but fish, and strange fish at that, in strange waters like Laguna Blanca. Fishing is a boy's right. When a man goes fishing he goes with the boy he was, back to the old mill-pond. I must fish in familiar waters, where I know the best holes, what time of day is best, what bait, and who the nibbler is about my hidden hook—hornpout, perch, pike or punkin-seed. When I was a child I fished as a child, and I have never had such fishing since. But there was never a trout in Cohansey Creek, or in Lupton's Pond, or up The Race to the Tumbling Dam.

II

I remember the scene vividly, and the good Doctor's dismay. It was back in my college days. "The ice went out of the Allegash to-day," read the telegram—from Rockwood on the shores of Moosehead, Maine. But anybody might have thought, from the commotion it caused in Rhode Island, that the ice-cap had melted off the top of the world, that the earth had got a hot-box and might burn up its pole.

The commotion was not general over the whole extent of Rhode Island, being confined to the city of Providence, within one house on Broad Street—in fact, where my friend the Doctor lived. But it was bad there. Such excitement over flies and rods and reels and camps and guides and speckled trout! Trout *are* pretty fish. But so are punkin-seeds.

This telegram was from the Doctor's old guide down in Maine. And it arrived in the nick of time. The Doctor was certainly in a bad way. A man who would behave like this must be in desperate need of fish. A day more of delay might prove fatal.

I was in need of fish, too, having been cooped up in college since September, in need of a mess of my own catching and frying—the very smell of the smoking pan gave me academic cramps. A little book-learning goes a long way with some persons. Dig worms I must, but such excitement as was on the Doctor never took hold of me, nor any such confusion of boots and books of flies and heaps of gear.

"Come on," he urged, "get your rods and flies! We'll go down to the Allegash"—this "Allegash" uttered as I never uttered home or heaven. Down to the Allegash—five hundred miles away for fishing!

I didn't understand. Besides, I had no flies. I always fished with worms. I had no rods, either. And what was the use of rods if one had a jack-knife to cut him a pole on the way to the pond? As for a reel, I did have a reel. It was one I had found, and I kept it for odds and ends of string. Fishing with a reel was too much like flying kites. Think of winding up a hornpout on a reel!

How the dear Doctor looked at me! Poor thing! I had never caught a trout? No, I never had. How could I when there were none in Cohansey Creek or in any pond I knew?

He was a good doctor. He could cure almost any ordinary case. But a man who had never caught a trout, and who harbored the notion that catching hornpout was fishing, that hornpout might really be fish and not reptiles, that man was hopeless. Nothing could be done for him.

Would I go if he paid the bill? He would lend me boots and rods and all the gear I needed.

He would pay me for my time, just to have the fun of seeing me catch my first real fish—a speckled trout!

Let no one offer me the woods of Maine, much less the Allegash. They are already mine. Cohansey Creek is not the Allegash. I wish the trail from Santa Barbara to Hingham ran by way of Maine and down the Allegash. But let no one tell me that a hornpout is a reptile; that the only real fishing is on the Allegash with rod and reel for speckled trout. He, who tells me that, was never a boy along the Delaware, or on the marshes of the Maurice River, or up and down Cohansey Creek, or among the mill-ponds of Salem and Cumberland and Cape May counties—ponds that are margined with magnolia and liquid-amber and wild persimmon trees.

I have been much in Maine since the dear Doctor insisted upon paying me to go. I have been fishing since, but not on the Allegash, nor am I likely to go here on Laguna Blanca. And I have caught trout, too, one trout, in the little brook which runs at the foot of Mullein Hill in Hingham.

That was a sentimental trout, and about as small as the law allows. That brook of mine in

Hingham is one from which Bradford Torrey took many a speckled beauty when he was a boy. I liked that Torrey boy. I had often been a-birding with him in his books—even for the wild swans here on Laguna Blanca; and it was perfectly natural that I should wish to go a-fishing with him in our joint brook. I went. But he was a shy boy and I was from New Jersey. I took one little trout; and though I have lived beside the brook these more than twenty years, Bradford and I have never gone fishing together since.

Every spring a fisherman beats up and down the brook. And every spring as I mend the fence or trim the apple trees I say to myself: "There, there's the shy, strange fisherman again. See him casting from behind the alder clumps! That's the Torrey boy! That's Bradford, re-turned to earth as he left it, in the guise of a grown man. But I know him. He would like a boy to fish the old brook with him. I will go up to the house and get one of the children's rods and join him." But it always turns out that I dig a can of worms and go over to Jacob's Pond for punkin-seeds and perch.

For I'm a shy lad, too, and no hand at all with a trout, having practiced all my boyhood on hornpout and perch and the like. I was trained, for instance, to sit down and fish. Trout fishermen walk up and down—a mighty poor way to fish, it seems to me. I was taught to throw a lead line or drop a cork into still, deep water, and then wait. All of that is wrong for trout. The trout fisherman never waits. He walks and casts, flicks a gaudy, humbug fly against a sun spot on a pool, as eager to hit the spot with the fly as to hit a trout with his hook.

I understand nothing of this. It is not fishing to me. I never wade and fish. I sit down and watch my taut line cut the current of the river, or follow my float on the black, burnished surface of the mill-pond, and wait and dream. Dreams are deep-water fish feeding near the bottom where it is still and dark.

Queer stubborn stuff, this soul-stuff of ours, that to this day I must get a can, must cut a pole, must find a stump beside a pond, or if I can a wharf by the river, in order to realize to the full the sweet sense of fishing. This is strange when any day in open season I might decorate myself with hip-boots, and jointed rod, and wicker creel,

and pretty flies with odd, old names, and, thus
accoutered, sally picturesquely up and down a
trout brook flowing past my very door! Or I
might slip down to Laguna Blanca and try the
spoon and spinner for a bass.

But I won't. A tepid-water bass, out of an
artificial lake, with a permit, is not my idea of a
good panfish. It is the fruit in California that
appeals to me, and the birds. I go out at dawn
every clear day and sweep the Santa Ynez peaks
for a flying condor; but I couldn't go fishing
here. Fishing is a boy's fun. There are boys in
California, for I have seen them; but somehow
society in California seems to me strangely
grown up. I could live here and die here like
most resigned Californians; but I shall doubtless
go back to Hingham before that, and, I hope,
back to Lupton's Pond and the waters of the
Cohansey.

III

I know such a good hole on the north side of
Lupton's Pond for hornpout! It is under a certain persimmon tree, the one which holds its
sugary fruit until January. A thick tangle of
green cat-brier climbs the old cedar near by.

Here the catbirds and the cardinals call. The swamp honeysuckle and tall magnolias flood the morning pond with perfume. From the slope under the persimmon tree I can look out over the meadows, out to the creek, where, its snowy sail half hidden by the banks, a sloop goes down on the flood tide to the bay. And the bay goes down under the wide summer sky to meet the sea.

Do you call such fishing tame? Then you do not know the excitement of being idle, as idle as the birds and fishes, with a chance to dream. I am not asleep. Far from it. The endless days I worked as a child, those are the sleep and the forgetting! I can remember vividly every hour I idled fishing, quick to see and hear and wonder— where the sloop was bound, going out with the tide into the bay.

It is when the pond is quiet that the water catches the color of the clouds, the swirl and wake of every swimming tail, and the image of the kingfisher rattling between the shores. So, too, when I am quiet with the pond, the fisher of me poised, a dragon-fly, upon the floating cork, the dreamer of me spread between two shores where drift the clouds and flitting shapes of birds and wings of loath winds lagging among the magnolias in the dark of the swamp. Not every sculling fin will curl the surface. But never am I so aware of all that stirs below and in the open around and over me, as when I watch, with fingers like the dragon-fly's upon my cork, my senses more than all the rest of me. For so I learned to fish and float and dream.

There were no trout brooks in my country. I never had the lively companionship of such a stream. Its clear cold waters never curled about my knees, nor did the quick strike of a fighting trout ever snap along my fishing pole. But I did know the deep water of the mill-pond, water so deep and dark that it was coffee-colored, stained by the glooms of the cedar swamps out of which it came.

Off at the head of the pond stretched the even, compact cedars in ordered multitudes; and here at the mill-dam gathered the still water, spreading in a thin, yellowish fan over the spillway; while down in front of the heavy dam, down on the creepy floor of the pond, in the monstrous shadows at the edge of the steep black slope lay a giant stump, a cuttle-fish stump, its rayed arms, round and slimy, feeling over the bottom and far down the steep into the dark.

Here I used to fish. Twelve or fourteen feet below the bobbing cork, close among the reaching arms of the stump, hung my hook. How often I would peer into the dark water only to make out dimly the long shadowy arms and the beaked head of the lurking stump! And I would shiver when the wind ruffled the surface at the way those dreadful arms would seem to writhe and twist and feel about for me.

Once they nearly got me. That was before I could swim. I let go of the dam one day and went straight down, straight down slowly, feet first, till I touched a cold arm of the cuttle fish. I felt the round rubbery tentacles whip about my body, drag me sidewise—and ——

What I next remembered was gravel stones and splinters, my brother Joe rolling me full of gravel stones and splinters on the footboards of the dam. Joe was some years older than I, and a very muskrat for swimming. When suddenly he looked around for me I was gone. But a dreadful line of bubbles told him where. And a gray blur on the bottom, a wavering faint shadow slipping out of the reach of the cuttle-fish and down the dark incline was what he dove for. Shadows can neither feel nor remember.

Joe could swim and dive like a seal. But I was as so much lead when he came up with me and got me to the dam. The old mill had long since fallen into ruin. The dam was far in from the road among the woods, and no one was passing. Joe had to lift me, limp and slippery, to the bank alone. And then he rolled me—till I was as full of hemlock splinters as a porcupine is of quills. I was likewise full of sand and gravel stones from the grit on the planks. Joe hadn't stopped to brush and smooth the planks. And I was mean enough to howl like a baboon when I came to and found Joe treating me so horridly.

Of course the experience soon made me a swimmer. Boys are not cured of the water by this sort of treatment. But it did give me a vivid feeling for uprooted pine stumps. And to this day, at the sight of one in the water, or tilted up for a fence on land, I think of cuttle-fish. And down in the coffee-colored depths of the mill-pond when the wind ruffles the surface, I can still see the monster curl its leathery arms and feel about for me.

If I have missed the beauty of the mountain and the laughter of the trout brook, I have had instead the wood-walled pond, the creek, the strong silent river with its mysterious tides and its windings through the infinite marshes to the bay. So I have not missed all. Not very much, perhaps.

It is a terrific thing to be a child anywhere. To have been wholly that thing which later is only the immortal part of us! We keep on being the child we were, no matter what manner of man we have become. The New Hampshire child will fish a trout brook to the end. The Wisconsin child will fish a sandy-shored lake for pike and muskellunge. The Louisiana child, with paddle and bateau, will find the slow lagoon and drop his hook. The California child, if he gets a permit, may try for bass behind the tules in Laguna Blanca. And that New Jersey child, take him where you will, teach him flies and reels and rods, and let him go a-fishing, that boy will dig him a can of worms, and cut him a pole, and, finding a mill-pond or a creek or a river, will sit down to fish and dream.

To be sure, I am sorry that I could not have had one little mountain out of all the Santa Ynez range in my salt marsh along the Delaware; and just one small cold New England brook tumbling down that California mountain alive with leaping trout. But I did have clouds above my marshes as high as mountains. And they looked like mountains. And what is one's imagination for? A mountain in the middle of a marsh would surely spoil the marsh. And why is not a wide salt marsh as lovely as a mountain?

I did know one twisting, darkling little stream that worked its way from Cubby Hollow to Lupton's Pond, which almost qualified for a trout brook. Only this was full of pike. With all its windings it might have been a mile long.

Time and time again have I traveled the length of that stream. In certain thick places among the ferns and briers and ropy grape vines I would have to go on all-fours, flat as a turtle to the ground, pushing my fish-pole ahead of me up to the edge of the magic pools.

That was an unusual fish-pole. Instead of hook and line there was fastened to the tip a fine copper wire with a slip-loop snare. It was queer fishing I did with that pole. But it was exciting.

The stream made a thousand turns, backed and eddied into a thousand tiny coves and bays through the thick of the swamp, and in every shadowy hole lurked a savage pike. There was

no fishing for them with hook and line here. No
grown-up angler ever crawled through that
jungle of dodder and cat-brier and chicken-
grape vines. Only a boy could penetrate it.
Under the roots of a big tupelo the stream had
dug a cave. A fallen log a few feet below had
banked the flow with sticks and leaves, backing
the water into a pool nearly waist deep. It is
twilight here even at high noon, but through the
shadows drop golden shafts of light, piercing the
limpid pool and patching the silvery, sandy floor
with gold. One yellow shaft strikes the tangled
overhanging roots of the tupelo and slants across
the green-gold body of a pike.

A big one! Sixteen inches if he is an inch! A
solitary, morose old monster who has held this
lair for years against all comers. And literally
held all of the comers! He lies back in among
the roots like a lurking submarine. And as I
look, there is a flash of something, a swirl in the
middle of the pool, a wake among the tupelo
roots, and back in his berth lies the pike, his long
raking hulk on even keel, and motionless, save
for the slow sculling of a pectoral fin.

I did not see him start or stop. But he went,
and he snapped up a five-inch pike as he swirled

at the middle of the hole. And here he lies, level, alert, the tiger of a three-foot jungle, waiting on the narrow trail from Cubby Hollow to Lupton's Pond.

But I also am on that narrow trail, motionless, level, alert. And I am as cunning as the tiger. Ah, but he *is* cunning, and as quick as light! This is not easy stalking. There are bushes between us. He lies beneath an arch of roots. And just how deep below the surface?

The hang of my snare is off. The loop is small to pass behind those angled jaws. Slowly I draw the long pole back, open the snood a trifle, bend it parallel to the pole, and slowly, invisibly move it forward till it hangs above the tiger's pointed head.

Hist! The pole will pass directly through the shaft of sunlight and cast a sharp shadow across the keen fierce face! If only a cloud would cover the swamp, or a breeze would scatter the pattern on the pool! Slowly, as if it were a thing growing in the bright spot, I shift the pole, its shadow creeping like the shadow of a dial in toward the long head with its underslung jaw.

The fin on my side just behind the gills quickens slightly. The long, torpedo hulk veers two points off. But my pole is as steady as the alder stems. Not my pulse. He feels the tremor through the water; knows something is impending; suspects, but does not understand.

Now my snare is out of angle. All the way back, inch by inch, I draw the length of the pole, twist the loop out a little to meet the new angle of the pike, then inch by inch work it forward once more, every muscle in my body taut, every nerve of singing steel.

A dozen caves and hidden passages border the pool. Once he is alarmed I shall not sight him again to-day. Shaped like a dart, built for speed, he can outflash the eye of the mink. But I have watched him closer than the mink. The wariest thing in water, he has so long lorded it over this uninvaded pool that fear is strange to him. He has never met an equal. Nothing that he could devour has ever entered these shades and left the shades alive.

With every nerve bent into the loop, every muscle strained along the pole, I lower the invisible snare into the water, barely clearing the torpedo head. It slips over the broad nose, past the unblinking, glittering eyes, and——

Did I get him? Look at the magnificent creature! No trout was ever built on such a keel, no bass with such a beam. And as for dots of red and gold, see the wavering welded lines down the burnished length of this Damascus dagger of the pool!

I have put away the gun forever. I do not dare to kill, and I have killed the desire to kill for sport. Living and letting live is better sport. But I am not consistent, for still I go fishing. And I would clear the banks of every river, sweeten the waters of every brook and lake and bayou, and stock them all with trout and pike and hornpout for every boy to go fishing.

I have not traveled far from boyhood, though I am far from the cool dark ponds of home. I now have Laguna Blanca and the Sierras in my front yard. But I shall not go fishing here. I shall return to the mill-pond and the marshes. And no boy who has the freedom of the wide salt marshes need cry for mountains, or wish his pike a spotted trout or weep because his hornpout is not a salmon.

CHAPTER NINE: NOT SO BLACK AS HIS FEATHERS

THIS is about Kratz's crow; but for all that I can see, Kratz's crow may be the very black rascal who pulls my corn, plugs my melons, picks my juicy pears; mocks, derides, and lords it over me by building his nest in the tallest white pine to be found on my place. *My* place? Where did I get that notion? Don't tell that to the crows. What a row there would be in *my* wood lot if this book should fall under the eye of *my* crows!

I am not certain that they can read. But I am certain that nothing goes on about Mullein Hill concerning them which they don't know. Big, black, cautious, impudent, canny, contentious, they are rather shady characters, the whole band of them, and very useful citizens.

No other word in ornithology, no other creature in my outdoors, is such a conflict of questions and answers as this word and creature "Crow." To-day I would destroy him. To-morrow I would defend him against all comers. While I am looking for him in the woods with a gun, he is helping himself to cutworms in my garden. He knows my plantings and harvestings, my up-risings and downsittings; the difference between firearms and garden tools; just how far my gun will carry; what time he can call me names, and when it is wise to treat me with respect. I don't know him quite so well; but though he wears the colors of the pirate, I am sure his soul is rather white.

Few lovers of birds will agree with me, how-ever. I do not agree with myself in nesting-time, for the crow is a robber of nests. He looks guilty and acts guilty all through May and June, sneaking and lurking about the trees, slipping silently in and out, perfectly conscious of his dirty work, and careful to avoid observation.

It is then that I sometimes snatch my gun and sally forth to destroy the crow tribe. But the news seems to go forth ahead of me. The woods are deep and wide and capable of hiding a good many crows. I have never killed a crow. Per-haps I ought to. But the birds they rob, like the robins, were more numerous this past summer than I have ever seen them in Hingham, as my cherry trees would swear to if they could testify.

Out of ten loaded cherry trees (there was a mulberry tree among them which I had planted especially for the birds), the robins, catbirds, and waxwings took a bushel for every quart I gathered. The crows are fond of cherries, too.

Suppose I shoot the crows because they rob the robins. Then I shall have to shoot the robins because they rob the cherry trees. And then—I have started something, something bad, which I had far better let alone. So I allow the crows to plug my melons and pilfer the nests, knowing it will last but a few weeks, when, for all the months to follow till the robins come back again, there will be loud cawing in the empty woods and continuous warfare waged against the insect enemies encamped round about Mullein Hill besieging me.

Who would hush that raucous cawing in the winter woods? Or wish his world without this strong, black figure, and the stronger,—I won't say blacker,—personality cloaked in this solemn judicial garb? No other bird looks so wise, not even the owl, or is so wise, as the crow. He invests all nature with intelligence. He comes nearest of all wild things to speaking the human language.

For he is wild and intends to be. A circling hen-hawk against the sky is so distant and alien as to seem like one of the stars. The fox is hidden, furtive, a creature of legend and story-book rather than of the real, near-by woods. Down by the kitchen steps sits the hop-toad in the twilight, thinking, thinking, but no one would give a penny for his thoughts. Bob-white comes up in the winter to feed with the chickens, half inclined to join the flock and leave his wild estate. Not so the crow.

Perhaps there are quail-like crows, but I have never seen them. In the dead of winter I have seen the birds down and out—dead from starvation and disease. Yet never did I see a humble crow. Bold and wary, always quick, the year around, to hail you, knowing as well as you where you are going and why, he watches curiously, comes prudently close, making no bones of his intense human interest, which, however, he tempers with extraordinary good sense, the kind we call "common," but which might well be called "crow."

"Hi, you black rascals!" I shout at them.

"Hi, you're black yourself!" they shout at me in turn. "We know a thing or two you'd like to know. Ha! Ha!" and off they go, leaving me sure that animals and men can talk together, at least that crows and men can understand each other. And this I can prove in the case of Kratz's crow.

Kratz had brought up several crows. So had I; and thereby made myself a general nuisance about home. But never did I inflict on my family a crow of such high craft and cunning as one that was brought up by my friend Kratz.

All house-raised crows which I have known or known about grew up as thieves. Domestication seems very bad for them. It was bright, shiny things particularly that tempted Kratz's crow. He grabbed the scissors from the sewing-basket, knives, forks, and spoons from the table, darting out of doors with them to the top of the house, thence to the top of the chimney, where he would drop them into the flue. Some one would be sure to shout at him, and he would turn on the chimney-top and squawk joyously back, giving every bit as good as he got, though sometimes it was the lady of the house who was wringing her hands and imploring him from below.

One day a pet crow that we had made off with grandmother's silver-bowed spectacles. Grand-

mother was a Quaker. Jim, the crow, had never
been to meeting. The "spirit moved" both of
them, Quaker and crow, and they had a very
lively time of testimony between them, one on
the ridge-pole, the other by the pump in the yard.

Another peculiarity tame crows seem to have
in common is their very marked preference for
a certain member of the family, following that
person about as faithfully as a dog. If a dog
happens to be in the family, rank jealously will
be sure to develop between the two animals where
this chosen person is concerned. This is not uncommon between cats and dogs, any attention, by
any member of the family, paid to the cat being
quite enough to make some sensitive dogs sick
with jealousy.

It is a mark of unusual mental power, I take
it, that such feelings can be entertained by a bird.
I have never known a tame crow and the pet
dog to get on sweetly together. There is constant bickering and nagging between them.

Kratz's mother was the particular object of
his crow's affections. The bird went with her
everywhere and helped her with everything. On
her head or shoulder, or tagging, stiffer than a
drum-major, along behind, he would follow from

sewing room to garden, taking a hand in all her tasks, talking a good deal, and none too modestly, of how indispensable he was.

You can imagine how much he helped when he got in with both feet among the spools and small wares, especially among the silks, of the sewing-table. Let a long-toed crow, with an inquisitive turn of mind, walk into your knitting, to say nothing of the sewing, and notice what happens.

Curiously enough, I never knew a mischief-maker to blame himself for the trouble he gets into, no matter what language he blames in. Kratz's crow was always in mischief, and always blaming the family in general for it. Instantly the thread got tangled in his toes, he would fall to squawking angrily, then get frightened and flop over helplessly for some one to unthread his miserable feet. He was exceedingly resourceful at inventing mischief, but most incapable at mending it.

His fondness for the mistress of the house caused him to become a kind of shadow to her. He attended her everywhere, but he was especially interested in her gardening. Old-fashioned mother that she was, she had a way of punishing the crow for his naughty tricks by using a small switch across his big black wings. He couldn't have felt it, but the noise was terrible enough, and he "would be good" instanter! At the first swish of the rod he would tumble down, turn over on his back, and, crying like a booby, stick up his black claws to ward off the blows. And this always worked. To switch him on his tender bare feet was more than the mother of Kratz and his crow could bear.

A fence with a swing gate ran between the dooryard and the Kratz's vegetable garden. One day Mrs. Kratz, with the crow as usual on her shoulder, went into the garden to pick snap beans. And the crow, as usual, began industriously to assist with the picking, doing exactly as he saw Mrs. Kratz doing. Only this time, because they were harder to get off, possibly, the crow would not touch the long, big beans, the ones that were ready to pick, but insisted upon picking the little ones.

He was told better. But crows do not always listen to instruction. He kept on picking little beans. Then he was well scolded and warned. But crows do not like scolding, and sometimes pay little heed to warnings. He kept on picking

little beans. He just didn't hear. It was such
fun picking little beans.

How eager he was! He would not put the
beans in the basket, however, but always in a
separate pile on the ground close beside it. Every
time the basket was moved, the busy crow would
start a fresh pile of his little beans. The beans
were plentiful, and his industry was very touching, so he was indulged like a spoiled child in his
whim until his mistress chanced to notice that he
was bringing not only beans, but also little cu-
cumbers and baby watermelons.

This would never do. It was quite terrible,
really! And snatching him in the act, she pulled
a weed and began to punish him. Over he went
on his back, cawing piteously, thrusting his
sprawling feet up to cover him.

That old trick had worked many a time. This
time the willful bird must truly be corrected.
Spare the rod and spoil the watermelon patch.
No, no! He must be taught to let the watermelons alone, or worse things than switches would
descend upon him, in harsher hands than hers.
So down upon the naked feet came the swishing,
stinging weed—once, twice, three times, before
the astonished crow fully grasped the situation.

He grasped it firmly then—in both tingling feet at once! With a kind of handspring from the flat of his back, he turned clear over in the air, struck out with both black wings, cleared that garden fence, and landed on the ridge-pole of the house before you could say "Kratz"! Then he turned right about and began to squall, everything he could think of and several things he never had thought of before, down at the laughing lady among the beans.

Out West they would say, "He got his needin's." And he didn't forget them, either. He forgave his mistress, as she forgave him. He continued to attend her everywhere—except through that garden gate. Bygones were bygones up to the garden gate. Let her enter here, and he left her shoulder, taking a position upon the gatepost, where he held forth, haranguing the lady most violently the while she picked beans or worked in the garden.

I know few, if any, parallels to such conduct among birds or animals under domestication, which seems to me to indicate a very high degree of intelligence for the crow. It also speaks of a very quick sympathy for his human neighbor and a readiness to meet him at least part of the way.

Once the ice is broken, the suspicions and animosities laid, the crow tribe seems ready to meet the tribe of man, making one world again of these two inimical worlds of crows and men.

Like a crow of mine, this crow of my friend Kratz showed a strong fear for all wild crows, his own relatives, about the farm. He would cry out in plain alarm at sight of them flying about, and would always retreat until they disappeared. Most wild things under domestication will return, if free, to the wilds for a mate. But spring came and went, and the crow, if he wanted a mate, did not seek her, though his wings were strong and free and all the sky was his.

It was the fear of death, I think, stronger in his keen consciousness than the desire for a mate, that restrained him. I have seen it several times (once in the case of a tame robin) that a bird, separated from his kind and brought up in human ways, has the mark of Cain put on him. Just what the sign is I should like to know. I have known a tamed wild duck and a tamed bluebird to return to their tribes and find mates; but such a renegade crow is the object of suspicion and fury on the part of the wild tribe. Let him try to come back, and he is set upon with violence and done to death.

An untimely accident took off Kratz's crow, leaving no opportunity to see later, when the call of the wild in his blood should be more urgent, if he would overcome his fears. We only know that to the end the sight and sound of his wild kin drove him croaking to shelter.

Here may be found a scrap of evidence, possibly, to justify that persistent old legend of crows court-martialing guilty members of their bands and picking them to death. Within a month, such a story, from an eyewitness, has come to me by way of an editor who wishes to publish the tale. It was all too circumstantial, too much like a story in my first reader at school. Yet who can say that such a thing may not go on within the councils of this black, powerful band of uncanny birds, who seem more than birds, both in their solemn demeanor and in their well-established ways.

In my neighborhood a small band of about a dozen crows live their gypsy life all winter. Spring finds them reduced to about three mated pairs, but whether reduced by death or agreement, dividing the land among them, I do not

know. I hear them cawing over in the thick
pines. All winter long they will be heard in loud,
confident talk over in the hollow woods. And I
shall see them all winter long, when few other
creatures care to stir abroad, flying strongly
against the leaden sky and stalking black upon
the deep drifted snow, their raven dress and
harsh, unlovely voices just the touch, in the
wintry landscape, of contrast and courage to give
one heart.

Say every evil thing you can against him, then
live through the winter with him as I do here on
Mullein Hill. He does plug melons and pull
sprouting corn. But read the government's report of his year-round warfare in defense of farm
and garden, and see what else he does. I have
caught him robbing nests of smaller birds, and is
not one robin of as much value as one crow? I
suppose it is. And I confess that I do not know
whether or not to kill the robber. But I do know
that when the nesting season is over I am always
glad I did not kill him; and I am sure that I
could lose almost any other bird from my world
out of doors and miss it less than I should miss
this constant, cantankerous, dubious character,
the crow.

CHAPTER TEN: THE JUNGLE TOURS THE TOWN

"A man's a fool to look at things too near:
They look back, and begin to cut up queer,"

soliloquizes William Vaughn Moody's philosopher at the menagerie,

"A little man in trousers, slightly jagged."

One does not need to be half drunk at a circus
for a touch of delirium. Nothing is more accusing, more nightmarish when one puts oneself behind the bars than wild things caged, on wheels,
and on show.

"Lost people, eyeing me with such a stare!
Patient, satiric, devilish, divine;
A gaze of hopeless envy, squalid care,
Hatred, and thwarted love, and dim despair."

I have never lost my small-boy wonder at the
caged beasts in the circus tent, though I grew up
long since and look upon them now with the sorrow of a man. What makes the menagerie tolerable still to me is the elephant, not the creature
going through its pathetic stunts, but going
through the town. I may be wrong, but take it

all together, and I've a sneaking notion that
circus life rather appeals to elephants. They are
observant, interested beasts, liking the shift and
go of the circus, and very much at home with
humankind.

In the Natural History Museum of Tufts College, Massachusetts, is to be seen all that remains
on earth of Jumbo, Barnum's great circus elephant, one of the most remarkable wild animals
ever brought into captivity by man. There his
huge bulk stands, just as in life, and it seems as
if the walls of the building must bulge and almost
give way from the very lock of pressure and the
feeling of crowding size exerted by the hulking
old monster.

Had there been no one with me I think I
might have spoken to him, so familiar, so friendly
did he look. And I had not seen him since I was
a boy! He used to know me in the old days when
his circus came to town. Many a pail of water
I have fetched for him, and many a wink and
knowing look has he given me in return. He was
almost the whole show to me.

Jumbo had a peculiar way of looking at me,
an understanding way, which, I think, may be
the way of all interested elephants. I can feel

to this day the kindly, penetrating eye of Jumbo *seeing* me, seeing all of me, through and through. He seemed to *look* me naked, body and soul. He knew my inmost mind, my intention before I had thought it out myself. And when he approved of me, when I knew that I could pass within the terrible circle of his might—under his belly, on his back, into the curl of his awful trunk, then I knew that all of my sins were forgiven, that my kingdom had come, for the Almighty, or Jumbo, was with me.

Explain it as you may, but Jumbo seemed a kind of Almighty to me. Yet he had the gentlest eye and the softest touching trunk. I can feel the tip of his finger-like trunk working around the edge of my ear and lifting my cap from my head, as if it were yesterday. I fear that the years, or my conscience, who knows, have made me too suspicious and fearful ever to trust an elephant to that extent again. I am sorry, too. But there are men who can.

I know of a certain surgeon, one of the most noted specialists in his field, who was recently called in to operate on the foot of a circus elephant. The great creature was in pain. It was an abscess in one of the front feet; and nothing had been found that relieved it. Matters grew rapidly worse. Trumpeting and swaying in pain, the elephant became nervous and excited, until even his keeper was afraid to approach him. Then the surgeon came. Yes; he could relieve him. But did he dare? Dare! Did ever the true doctor in the face of pain or death ask himself if he dared? He came up to the dangerous patient, two of whose legs were chained to heavy stakes, and spoke to him. He showed him the knife, the cleansing fluids, the bandages, and told him it would hurt, but only for an instant.

And the elephant understood every word that was said to him. Or else he read the character and understood the friendly, fearless spirit of the man before him. He quieted immediately. The doctor bent under the vast hanging head and bade the beast to pick up his sore foot. As the ponderous foot came up and back on the surgeon's knee a nervous tremor shook the mountainous form of the beast. It shook the doctor, too. As he washed the swollen, fevered spot, and reached for his lancet, he felt the sensitive tip of the long trunk curl like a finger about and lightly grip the hair on his bent head.

It was a fearful moment. But the touch

of the trunk was confiding like the grasp of a child's hand. The knife shot with a flame of fire through the throbbing lump. There was a spurt of blood, a groan of pain, a quiver through the mighty frame, and then, as the easing like a soothing wave swept the huge body, the trunk let go its hold on the surgeon's hair and, thrown aloft, swung wildly to the loud trumpetings of relief and joy.

I am no longer a schoolboy, as I have intimated, except in heart. It has been ten years since I went to a circus. But I see the big show come in at the railroad station if I can. I love the street parade. Eight dappled horses drawing a rumbling van is a thrilling sight to me. So are the polar bears, and things. But most of all I hurry to the street to see the elephants shamble by.

Were I to join the circus, I should want to be the keeper of the biggest elephant. If ever I come home a conquering hero, I shall come according to early dreams, riding all alone through the streets of my native town, on the sagging, heaving head of an elephant, with only an ankus in my hand to prove my complete conquest.

And I'm a grown man, a college professor, and

talking like this! I confess it. And I confess that, to this day, every huge, hulking elephant rolling through the street in a circus parade looks at me out of the corner of his little eye as if he had some deep secret he would tell me, could I only come out to the big tent at the circus grounds and listen.

Perhaps I shall never know what the secret is. There is always a crowd under the big tent. Perhaps it is a jungle secret; and perhaps the look in his eye means, "If only we could escape from all of these people, and from all this noise and show and confusion, back to the wide, deep quiet of the jungle, just you and I, brother, I would tell you the riddle of life."

Before the days of Jumbo, there used to come every year an old elephant to our town, whose name I never knew, but for whom I have carried many a pail of water. He was a contented, good-natured giant, a very king to me, and I served him like a slave. On this particular May day the sun was hot, real jungle weather, and the mighty old monarch from the jungle was in the best of humor. But he had returned from the parade enormously thirsty. Bucket after bucket of water he sucked up as though they were only so many glasses of lemonade. It made me thirsty just to see him drink. And it made me thirstier to swing those heavy buckets across the wide circus grounds to the tent. All of which the elephant saw, and for all of which he was very sorry.

So, at last, when I had filled him up, and stood wiping the sweat from my admiring brow, that old rogue quietly sipped up the last bucketful, and swinging a little in my direction, blew the whole of it over me, drenching me most completely and most thoroughly, ducking me from head to foot!

And then he laughed. Perhaps an elephant can't laugh. But this one could. And I think he did. And then he squealed. Then all the other elephants squealed. And all the boys who hadn't been soaked squealed. And everybody in the big tent squealed in wild delight at sight of me, wet as a drowned rat! But I was cooled off now, and refreshed, and in no danger at all from sunstroke.

But I didn't care. At least I don't care now, after these more than forty years. And I would carry water again, and run the risk of another ducking, if that were the only way I could get into the circus.

I knew most of the circus elephants in those days, but there was no other elephant like Jumbo. He was the biggest elephant that ever came to America, and the gentlest elephant, and the most intelligent, too. He was killed on the railroad many years ago; but thousands of persons still remember him, and the jaunts they had on his heaving back under the circus tent.

While he was still alive, and spending his winters in the circus quarters at Bridgeport, Conn., my friend, the animal painter, Mr. Alexander Pope, used to see much of him. One day he saw Jumbo do something which showed the elephant had not only intelligence, but also patience of more than human quality.

Mr. Pope had been painting the lions that day and was crossing the yard when he came upon Jumbo helping to move some freight cars about the tracks. The circus people used Jumbo instead of an engine. All the big pachyderm had to do was to get behind the heaviest freight car and lean his head against it kindly, and that car would seem to know what was wanted of it and would roll off just like a baby carriage.

On this particular day Jumbo had been told to go down the track to a single freight car, which

stood in the middle of the yard, and push it along
to one of the sheds. Lumbering down to the car,
Jumbo swung in and looked the job over. His
keeper came up and spoke to him, Jumbo still
quietly studying his car.

It was a circus special, a high, heavy car of
gaudy gilt and carving, but it was empty and
mere child's work for a real elephant. Why
didn't they give him one to play with that was
full of pig iron or loaded with about six blood-
sweating hippopotamuses? And he came about
as some ocean liner in behind the car so as to push
directly, moved up close, lowered his head, and
very slowly, very gently leaned against the un-
offending car.

The car leaned back against Jumbo. The big
elephant was not pushing a pound. He acted as
if he were feeling about the carving for nails, or
scratching his big head, so gingerly did he bear
on. But this was his usual manner, only this
time the car did not move, not a single inch.

"Come, come!" said the keeper, "get busy
there! Don't try to *think* this car along. Get at
the go-cart and push."

But Jumbo very evidently was thinking. However, he was used to minding that voice, and drop-

ping his head a little lower, he made believe to push. The car stood still.

"*Jumbo!*" called the keeper, sharply. "Stop your fooling, you lazy lubber, and dig in your toes!"

Instead of digging in his toes Jumbo wig-wagged his big left ear, rolled a wise little eye around, and without budging, looked hard at his keeper. But the keeper was not taking orders from Jumbo, he was giving them to him. Besides, the keeper was now thoroughly impatient. There had been enough nonsense. And he said some quick things which Jumbo clearly understood.

The great head dropped a bit lower still down the end of the car. The heaped-up shoulders worked forward and up a little higher. The two tublike front feet shifted just a little more se-curely between the cross-ties of the track. And Jumbo really pushed, but not hard. The car stood still.

What had come over the stubborn beast, any-way! And the unobservant keeper, now thor-oughly angry, stepped up to the flapping ears and, shouting into them, struck one of them a stinging blow with his iron hook, yelling, "*Push!*"

Then Jumbo knew what was expected of him.

The blow of the iron hook was received without protest or any show of surly spirit. The keeper was human and a fool, that was all. Lowering his head now in earnest, all four of his mammoth feet firm among the ties, Jumbo bent forward, shoulders down, hips humped, and piling all his mountainous body up behind his head, *pushed*.

There was just an instant of suspense, when with a splintering crash his head went through the planking as the whole gilded end of the car gave way.

Then the splendid creature drew back, pulled his head out of the wreckage, and, swinging about toward his keeper, eyed him quietly as he plainly said: "There, I told you so, you poor boob. Why didn't you know enough to take the brakes off this car?"

CHAPTER ELEVEN: THE BIRD-BANDER

IN JUNE of this year (1925), half a dozen authorized bird-banders, a son of mine among them, camped for three days on Cape Cod in order to band the young black-crowned night herons in the famous rookery at Sandy Neck, Barnstable, probably the largest rookery of these birds in this part of the country. The black-crowned night herons build in trees, and the birds of this colony occupy an extensive grove of pitch pines among the mosquitoes and sand dunes on the shores of the cape. When the banders arrived in the third week of June the nestlings were about ready to fly.

The banding was not sweet work—though not a bander would allow me to say that. It was dirty, sweaty, smelly work they all agreed, but as for being sweet—why have they promised me the experience next season, as the greatest of favors, if it is not sweet? Climbing around all day in the tops of pine trees, out on cracking limbs and among heron nests, is hard work, too, and dan-

gerous for fathers of grown sons. But a bird-
bander is an enthusiast, whatever else he may
accidentally be, so don't worry him about a little
thing like a broken neck or arm.

Not every young bird in the rookery received
an anklet. But when the party was over 1,433
nestlings had been tagged, each with his own
registered number, which was straightway recorded at Washington with the Biological Survey. And these hundreds of tagged birds, together with hundreds of the three previous seasons, are now at large, winging about the country
and making history for the Sandy Neck Colony
and for the whole black-crowned night heron
tribe, and for these banders very especially.

On each neat, rustless, easy band of aluminum
is stamped a serial number, and along with it, for
the bander, there is a record card bearing the
same number. As soon as the band is closed
about the bird's leg, the species of the bird, the
bander's name, the place, and date are entered on
the corresponding card and sent for filing to the
federal authorities at Washington. Then if that
bird is later shot, or found dead, or taken in a
bander's trap, it is reported by number to Washington, and the office there reports back to the

original bander that black-crowned night heron
No. 335391 was picked up dead in East Brown-
field, Maine, September 28, 1925, by Lolita
Crabtree—an actual report which has just come
in of one of the herons banded by my son in June.
Thus the circle is closed, and the wanderings
of that particular bird, short indeed for No. 335-
391, immensely far and thrilling for others, is
known from his pine-tree cradle to his down-east
grave.

Only a small percentage of these 1,433 banded
birds will ever again be touched by human hands.
Only a few of the persons killing or finding them
will be intelligent enough to read the bands with
understanding, and interested enough to send
the figures on to Washington. Yet the country
over is pretty much alive to the meaning of the
birds, and the banders themselves are no small
company, their scattered stations covering the
entire land.

A tremendous amount of chance is inevitable
with such work, and consequently a corresponding amount of adventure and romance. Truth
moves ahead with missteps mostly. The actual
reports back to the bander have been more than
the hazards promise, and each of them is a tale

worth telling, and a fact worth recording in the
little Odyssey of the bird, and in the wider wanderings of its family and race.

One of the young birds, No. 335683, was early
picked up a few miles east of its rookery at Ply-
mouth, Massachusetts; No. 335391 was found
dead in Maine. The young birds, instead of moving south, are first apparently, moving east.
Others have been and doubtless will be reported
from Canada—going north in the fall! This is
astonishing, and one must ask, Why do these
young birds go on a perilous journey north in the
short interval between leaving the rookery and
the forced journey south for the winter?

The numbered bands about the herons' legs
may not answer that question for us, nor many
another which they shall cause us to ask. But
what interesting questions these are! Questions
that are themselves more than knowledge, being
incentives to research. Nevertheless, 1,433 young
birds thus tagged and traceable in their unim-
peded movements before love affairs and family
duties come upon to tame and colonize them, are
sure, among them all to compose something of a
life story and write it with an indelible quill upon
the blank and fluttering pages of the air.

I began to band birds in 1912, in Oregon, before the days of the trap and the official help from Washington, and when the work was almost entirely confined to nestlings. It is now well established that the mortality among young birds before they are done with parental care reaches an appalling fifty per cent or more. How futile to band that foredoomed multitude! It could lead to almost nothing, and we banders of that early time very largely abandoned the work.

Little did we dream then of a nationally organized and legally authorized association of bird-banders, covering the country. And just as little did we dream of trapping old birds of many kinds, and in sufficient numbers to make their tagging of scientific value; actually opening up a new field for bird study, giving new life and zest to the old science of ornithology.

The little learned are always asking what important new facts can at this late day be discovered about anything—the well-worn theme of birds particularly? "More than five hundred thousand facts," says a recent writer, "about the migration of birds have been discovered within the last twenty-five years." A beginner in bird-study might be forgiven if he asked whether there is still a possible fact left undiscovered about migration.

Now here come the bird-banders over the top with batteries of new facts and barrages of fresh questions, taking the old intrenched science by storm. It is just such an assault as took place when we dropped ornithology by gun and took up ornithology by camera.

With banding stations up and down the grand trunk routes of the migrating birds it is going to be possible to tag my phœbe in Hingham and discover: 1, just how fast he travels daily on his annual round trip; 2, when he travels most, by night or day; 3, what stop-overs, if any, he makes, and where and why; 4, where he passes the winter and what he does there; 5, when he starts back for Hingham and when he arrives; 6, if he is the selfsame phœbe who built under the roof last season; 7, whether or not he has the same mate as last year or has picked up another on the way; 8, whether he or she comes first in the spring; 9, how many years he continues to return; 10, if any of the banded young from under the roof return to this neighborhood, or where they do go; 11, do the mated pair stick it out together all summer in spite of their three broods; and 12, will the bird return south in the fall by the route of the previous year?

So we could continue with more than this single dozen of questions about the personal ways of this particular phœbe, with answers involving not only the adventure and truth of this individual bird, but also the story of his tribe.

What if, twenty-two years ago, I had banded the pair of phœbes nesting under my pigpen? What a life story, possibly, I could now unfold! The love affairs, the family affairs, the goings and comings in the spring and fall! I had rather read the actual events of this strange tale set down in notes, than the wildest thriller a story-teller could invent.

I found a pair of phœbes nesting on a stringer under the roof of the pigpen when I moved to Mullein Hill in 1902. Spring after spring they returned to the apple-limb bracket which I nailed up for them, until the spring of 1914, when in rebuilding the pen I thoughtlessly closed the little square window on the north, blocking the birds' through passage in the pen. I did not know what offense I had given until I found the pair with a new nest on the ice-house. Here the cats and squirrels raided them, and again they moved, this time up under the coving of the house roof beyond the reach of even the squirrels. And here they now are.

Here they *were,* I should say, the very same pair, so far as I could tell, until last summer, when, during incubation time, I picked up one of the two birds dead upon the lawn. But what do I know of this story, and of the whole long story? Only that for fourteen Aprils in succession a pair of phœbes had a nest in the same spot under the pigpen, and that since then a pair have built in one spot under the eaves of the house!

How I should like to know it all! But there is not a single feather on their normal bodies to distinguish these two birds from any others of their kind, and no records of their lives after the nesting season is done. How the numbered bands, however, might have told what I so much desire to know!

A bird-bander is something of a small town social reporter along with his more important scientific work. Something of a scandal-monger, too, as witness the unsavory things he is saying about Jenny Wren! We have long suspected things in Wrendom, but really the carryings-on of wren husbands and wives, the way they are swapped and bargained for, is something terrible even among the wrens. "For better or for worse, till death do us part," either does not enter into their marriage contract, or else is openly flouted —all of which is proved and more than proved when they are wedded by two rings of aluminum stamped with registered numbers!

Things are picked up and confirmed by the banders which had been hardly more than rumors heretofore. One day, for instance (it was January 25, 1923), twenty-three juncos were banded at Mr. Lawrence B. Fletcher's station in Cohasset, Massachusetts, nineteen of these taken at one time out of the trap together. A year passed. In February, 1924, twelve juncos entered this same automatic trap between 10 A.M. and 11.30 A.M., and *six of them were six of those nineteen that had been in that very trap together a year and ten days before.*

This sounds like a fish story, not a bird story. But these six juncos wore their numbered bands given them by Mr. Fletcher's hand in this spot, out of this trap, the year before. They were here together. They had evidently traveled down from the north together, and the strong presumption is that they had been living and nesting near

together during the summer as a colony, or
neighborhood, somewhere farther east and north.

What a pleasing fancy!—fact, rather, and as
interesting as it is pleasing. Who knew that
birds, not bound by family ties like a covey of
quail, or brought into companies by a sandbank
as certain swallows are, or by some strip of beach
where terns and plovers nest—who knew, I say,
that birds as free to wander as juncos are, nest
near together? Sing for each other as well as
for their mates? And maintain a kind of village
life? We knew they band together for travel,
and keep close together for food and protection
in the cold and snowy winter. But it is a new
light upon their social instincts to know that when
life and love are calling in the spring, and each
one is singling out his mate, still they keep together, all the way back down lovers' lane from
Cohasset into Canada.

Here is another new glimpse: "Case No. 3"
was a junco who wore band No. 75429, bestowed
upon him January 10 at 4.15 P.M.

On January 14 he was again captured, at 5
A.M., and from that day on until April 27 he was
retaken in this same trap just twenty times! He
may have been dreadfully frightened on January

10 at finding himself trapped and a big human hand closing over him. But he utterly forgot it in four days' time, entering the trap again, to be again the victim of the hand. It seemed to take him fifteen days to get over his fright this time. But how completely he recovered! He went back into the trap January 29, February 1, 7 (twice), 9, 10, and on the 11th had the nerve to get himself caught three times! Each time he was gobbled up by the big paw, his number taken, his little head gently stroked as the fingers crooked about him slowly opened until they were as wide as the bending friendly sky.

Perfect love, it is said, casteth out fear, and "Case No. 3" seems a good illustration of it.

"Case No. 1" is to illustrate a different thing— the constancy of life, even of free, winged life, and how bound it is to the soil.

> "East, west,
> Hame's best"

is a universal sentiment, as binding with birds as with men. Case No. 1 was a song sparrow who was tagged May 28, 1921, by Mr. Fletcher with anklet number 11006. He was found in the trap again on May 31, and on June 5, 6, 7, and 16, when he disappeared. A year later, on May 13,

he turned up in the trap wearing his number
11006. Eight times that summer he was taken
from the trap. Then he again disappeared. A
year later, on April 20 (1923), at 3.45 P.M., a
song sparrow was having a free supper in the
bird trap, and on his leg was band numbered
11006. Nineteen times that summer he repeated
this foolish feeding in the trap and this getting
himself in print. After that he went away and
there is no record of him since.

These are small matters, to be sure, if anything of life and truth can be small. There are
larger matters, possibly, longer matters, at least,
of migration that bird-banding is helping to make
scientifically sure. Formerly these facts were
picked up haphazardly, accidentally often, quite
by chance.

I cannot vouch for the exact details of the following story, which I am taking from *Our Dumb
Animals* (a most reliable paper), but while the
account is vague as to the species of plover, the
rest of the story is circumstantial to the last degree, and vividly illustrates the accidental nature
of our past knowledge of bird migration.

Says the writer: "For a number of years a
colony of laborers were stationed on Lysan Is-

land, a low, sandy bit of land about two and a half miles long by a mile wide, and one of the isles which form the Hawaiian Bird Reservation. One autumn a handsome male plover began to roost each night on a sand mound a dozen or so yards from the manager's hut. Mr. Max Schlemmer was in charge of the colony at that time. One day he saw the bird fluttering about on the sand, apparently unable to fly. Catching the plover, the manager discovered that one of the bird's legs was broken. He amputated the leg at the fracture and then released the bird. The stump soon healed perfectly.

"The plover continued to return each night to roost on the sand mound near the manager's hut. His having only one leg caused him to become an object of much interest to the handful of men on the isle, and they soon came to call him 'Stump-leg.' He grew to be exceptionally tame.

"Spring came, and one night Stump-leg did not return to his roost . . . the instinct of migration had called him northward with the rest of the birds. The manager, a seafaring man, kept a log-book at all times, and in it he recorded the departure of Stump-leg. He and his men did not expect to see their feathered neighbor again.

"One morning in the first part of the following autumn, however, Stump-leg was discovered sitting on his sand-mound roost. Every one was genuinely excited by the return of the one-legged plover. His arrival was recorded in the log.

"Stump-leg's return was complete proof that the flight from the mainland out to the Hawaiian Islands was made more than once by the same bird. Since Stump-leg had done so, there was no doubt that thousands of other birds had, too.

"Every member of the colony now regarded the one-legged plover somewhat as a hero. He was looked upon as both an extremely able seaman and more than a master navigator.

"Four more times did Stump-leg make the long, weary voyage out to Lysan Island, spend the winter there, and then set out to return to the mainland and go north into Alaska. He arrived at the island on nearly the same date each year; and every spring he left with the same punctuality. His arrival and departure were always recorded in the log.

"Finally there came an autumn when the other birds returned, but he did not. Autumn lengthened into winter, but still the one-legged plover did not appear on the isle. Then Mr. Schlemmer and his men knew that Stump-leg must be dead."

A wonderful story! But by what a strange accident it was found and put together—an amputated leg! Science that has to travel on stump-legs cannot hope to travel far nor very fast. For one stump-leg we are now following thousands of banded legs, numbered and known in Washington, in Europe, and in distant parts of the world. And for interested workmen on Lysan we have stations with observers all the way from far-off Lysan to the tundras of Alaska reporting the plover's passage, recording the stages of his daring, lonely flight, and marking, now and then, his lonely fall.

But there is one bird which has never been known to fall, or rather, whose flight we have never been able to follow throughout its mysterious annual course. Where does the chimney swift pass the winter? Old Gilbert White, of Selborne, asked that question many years ago. We are still asking it. For centuries this abundant bird has dodged the eyes of all the watching world and utterly disappeared in winter, not one bird, not a few birds, but millions of them, only to come rattling over the housetops and dropping into our chimneys with the coming summer.

It seems incredible. With keen observers covering every plain and mountain peak around the world, how can anything so large as a swift, and in such numbers, drop out of sight, and stay out of sight, for months together? This is not a very large world. It is a very well peopled and most persistently explored world. Yet why don't we uncover this hidden country of the swift?

I have seen these birds by the thousands. I know one vast chimney along the Maurice River over which a cloud of migrating swifts would hover and settle into for a night. They must have incrusted the sooty walls and clung to one another's backs until the great black flue was choked with them. But they would be gone by morning, consumed as by fire, the fluttering cloud of the evening as so much drifting smoke that had faded into the sky.

Now we are banding them, multitudes of them. But to what end? If he has been able to hide his body for so long he certainly can continue to hide his banded leg. If only Arachne, the spider, would spin us a silken thread to fasten to the aluminum band! Then we might follow the little spook and find, when he slips from his chimney flue, if really he has witch's wings and flies off to the mountains of the moon.

I do not know who shall make for us this interesting discovery. But I do know that fame awaits the finder of this mysterious winter kingdom of the swifts, as lost to us as the fabled lost Atlantis, somewhere back of the south wind, possibly, if any bander dare travel into realms so strange and far away.

CHAPTER TWELVE: QUAIL IN HINGHAM

OUT OF the swampy tangle in the hollow I hear the morning notes of the wood thrush, a shy, hidden minstrel, the voice of the woods at prayer. Below in the open meadow tumbling cataracts of bobolinking come tinkling up to me. I saw two male bobolinks over the meadow yesterday, just returned from their winter journey, and newly wed, and dangerously happy—a human view! They could not stay down in the lush grass for a whole minute together, so bubbling were their spirits, so buoyant were their souls with song.

All the air this morning is lively with cries and calls, for this is early June, the lovely din close caught to earth, where everything seems listening except these singing birds. And now the quiet speaks, or seems to me to speak, so unaccustomed am I to the call of the quail. High above the nearer notes, and off beyond the meadow under the wall of the woods, I hear the clean-cut whistle, "Bob-white! Bob-white!"—round and tender, each throbbing syllable a clear pure curve of melody, almost of color, as it arches the meadow and falls upon my ear.

Yesterday a thunder shower, a great wind, and a blazing sunset fought a gorgeous, but a drawn, battle around the horizon for the close of the day. This morning the three warring forces have withdrawn and lie hidden, each waiting for the other to attack. Anything in the way of weather may happen. Not a whiff of wind stirs. The sun might still be back of China. The smoky sky at any moment could rumble with muffled thunder. And such close silence is lying upon the fields that I can hear two workmen talking nearly half a mile away.

Out of this silence ascends the chant of the wood thrush; down upon it spatter and splash the lyrics of the bobolinks, but speaking it, the tenderness and tragedy of it, comes the call of the quail.

No, these are only my own tongues speaking, not the notes of birds. For all three are singing love songs, the quail's song associated in my memory since childhood with harvest-time and the gold of the year; but latterly, and for a long time now, significant of silence and things pass-

ing, so seldom have I heard the sweet call across
these Hingham fields. Only three seasons out of
twenty have the quail called on my side of
Hingham.

The birds were once abundant here, but there
are none at all now except as an occasional pair,
coming out from the sanctuary on the opposite
side of the town, nest and bring off a covey. Then
the open season comes and hunters come from all
sides of the town. There are many regions South
and West where bob-white is abundant, and with
the protection now offered them can be main-
tained in numbers. They are hardy creatures,
except in localities of snowy, crusted winters;
they are prolific, too, the average covey numbering at least a dozen, the stock capable of terrific
depletion, and as a race in no imminent danger of
extinction.

I wish I believed that. But I am neighbor
to the last colony of heath hen, near relatives of
the quail, and once as plentiful over New England, and far beyond New England, but now, in
spite of earnest protection, fading rapidly before
our eyes, the splendid race reduced to a tragic
score of birds. As with certain failing plants,
fate itself seems to be against the birds. Their

day is done, their departure is at hand, no matter what the help they receive, as if the intricate and multitudinous conditions making up their environment, once friendly, now spelled their doom. Help (and we could have helped!) came too late.

Except for the protection of our Hingham sanctuary I should in all probability never hear bob-white whistling from the gray stone fences on my side of the town again, though this is perfect quail country, and he is protected here by law. The trouble is he is also slaughtered by law, the law never knowing which two birds are the last mated pair.

Nor is there any way of knowing that the fate overtaking the heath hen shall not come upon the quail. Not long shall we wait for the last act in that tragedy which all lovers of bird life are watching move across the little stage on Martha's Vineyard. The beach plum shall bloom and the sweet-fern continue to scent the summer air. There may not be less of *life* on Martha's Vineyard, but soon there shall be one less *form* of life on Martha's Vineyard and in all the world; with the passing of the heath hen, one less living race,

unique, inimitable, a beautiful shape gone into
the shapeless void.

We have moving pictures of the heath hen,
and mounted specimens. Some society may
erect a monument on the island to mark the spot
and the date of the needless end. Small comfort
in that.

> "A rose to the living is more
> Than sumptuous wreaths to the dead."

We did give the bird sanctuary. But the sea
winds over Martha's Vineyard whisper as they
pass, "Too late! Too late!"

Bob-white needs sanctuary and needs it now.
Hardier, it may be, than the heath hen, and
readier for human associations, bob-white might
forever hold his own. It is the family we must
save while it is still a family, spread as a family
and conscious that it is a family. Reduce a
family to a handful of individuals, and its spirit
is broken. Let a species begin to slip and something racial seems to overtake it—a loss of heart
and vital strength and natural instincts; less
mating occurs; fewer young are raised; and, conquered as a race, seems as a race to pass within
the shadow of its doom.

The singing of the bobolinks is the merrier, I think, for the law New Jersey has recently passed placing these birds upon the protected list. I was a New Jersey boy, loving the tall reeds of the river flats as much as the bobolinks, where in autumn I have seen the birds slaughtered by the thousands. As soon as the big reeds began to ripen the bobolinks—or "reedbirds" or "rice-birds," as we called them—moving south, would swoop down upon the meadows, and down upon the birds would swoop the city gunners, from Philadelphia mostly. The destruction was awful. That is forbidden now.

Behind this new law, however, and stronger than the law, is the growing sympathy and understanding of the people. Much as we need such laws, they are worse than null unless those who write them upon the statute books first write them upon their hearts. Love and law will save the bobolinks. It is love that knows his song, knows his story, knows his significance in a world of men and meadows. This is spirit—which makes the letter of the law alive.

Every reason for protecting the bobolink or any bird is a reason for protecting the quail. Only the beauty of his scaling flight—a perfect mark—and his plump body can be advanced for killing him. He ought at once to be taken from the game-bird class, except in private preserves, and placed securely among the insect-eaters as the friend of man.

Bob-white is a seed-eater, a prodigious seed-eater, there is no denying that, and according to Mrs. Margaret Morse Nice in Vol. III, No. 3, of the *Journal of Economic Entomology,* a single bob-white in a single day has been known to eat of barnyard grass 2,500 seeds; beggar ticks, 1,400; black mustard, 2,500; burdock, 600; crab grass, 2,000; curled dock, 4,175; dodder, 1,560; evening primrose, 10,000; lamb's quarter, 15,000; milkweed, 770; pepper grass, 2,400; pigweed, 12,000; plantain, 12,500; rabbit's-foot clover, 30,000; round-headed bush clover, 1,800; smartweed, 2,250; white vervain, 18,750; water smartweed, 2,000; besides—but this leaves no reasonable doubt of bob-white's being something of a seed-eater.

For a day of three square meals, 122,205 seeds, and every seed of them a pest! Besides these I was starting to say, bob-white is the enemy of 145 species of injurious insects, including cutworms.

And his appetite for trouble of this sort is as immeasurable as it is for troubling seeds.

A friend of mine in Illinois came recently upon a hen quail, surrounded by numerous chicks, and watched her climb the tall weeds to shake down the chinch bugs infesting them to her devouring brood. Some of the weeds and grass she bent down where the chicks could pick the bugs off, scratching hard to provide for her family, but scratching harder still, though she recked little of it, to provide for the family of my farmer friend—and myself.

Many a time I have followed the tracks of the quail in a freshly cultivated potato patch where they have run about with havoc to the beetles. Paris green will do for the beetles, to be sure, but Paris green is expensive and dangerous. The immense economic waste borne annually by the nation on account of insects staggers the multiplication table. It is our greatest single loss. Over against these insect enemies nature has set the birds. This is a bug-bitten, worm-eaten, louse-infested world. But what light the quail throws upon the situation! He was constructed to take care of 145 species of them. And the comfort of knowing that a single flicker has a

counted record of 1,000 chinch bugs for a meal;
that a cuckoo has been seen to devour "250 tent
caterpillars when disturbed in the *midst* of a
meal"; and that in forty minutes a Maryland
yellow-throat was observed to stow away a total
of 3,500 plant lice!

These are thrilling, no less than comforting,
figures, or would be if only there were quails and
cuckoos and flickers and Maryland yellow-
throats enough. And we still have the chance
to make them enough. But let the slaughter
continue and not only shall worms destroy our
bodies in the grave, but they shall crawl over the
land of the living and eat up the world.

Bob-white is "the most marvelous engine of
destruction for the smaller pests of the farm ever
put together of flesh and blood," says one of our
scientists. And what a marvel, what a triumph
of anatomical engineering is his competent, compact body! Is there known a better constitution
than his?

The bird is literally born with his boots on.
The Illinois friend who told me the chinch-bug
story came upon a quail's nest in one of his wheat
fields, and carefully mowed around the spot,
hoping to spare the eggs. Passing that way a

few days later, he stopped to take a look at the
nest. The sun was beating down upon the unprotected eggs, only a few of which were left.
The birds had abandoned their home, he thought.
Probably a fox or skunk had raided it.

But as he looked he imagined that one of the
eggs stirred a little. A most mysterious thing!
He came nearer and watched. The egg moved
again, and he saw the pointed tip of a beak crack
through the shell, and rapidly, right around in a
circle, like some automatic punching machine
operating from within, cut the shell in two.
There was a kick, and a flop, and a popping,
panting baby quail standing in the fierce sun-
shine. He caught his breath, took a squint at his
hatcher in the sky and hiked for cover, still damp
from the shell.

Here is a bird that needs nothing but a chance,
and less than half a chance at that. Vitality such
as his needs food only, and we have the weeds and
bugs. This strength and courage is characteristic of the family. The plumed quail, or valley
quail of California, like bob-white, begins to
scratch for himself almost before he is hatched.
He is "on his mark" and ready to jump in the
shell.

A pair of valley quail built a nest in a window box among the plants some six or eight feet from the ground. It chanced that the people of the house were ardent bird-lovers, and in their delight made the couple welcome to the window, the while they kept a most unneighborly watch upon the exquisite domestic affairs behind the big pane of glass.

As the time arrived for the eggs to hatch everybody was concerned about the sheer drop from the window box to the ground. How would the chicks get down? Except for a small rosebush a bit to one side there was nothing beneath the window to break the fall. Would the mother help them—on her back, as tradition has it, or in her mouth as a cat carries her kittens?

There is a vast difference between a baby quail and a kitten. The first scatter-brain chick to hatch jumped right out of the box, to the horror of the watchers, without so much as a look beneath to see how far he might descend or where he might land, and fluttering his stub wings like tiny fins, hit the ground with a thud, bounced up, got his feet, and staggered off—smashing home ties with the world's record for speed.

These birds are not of the apron-string class.

Two or three more of the brood took the same sudden departure from the nest in the box, but most of the covey stayed a moment to reconnoiter, discovered the rose-bush under the corner of the window sill, and dropped off into it, tumbling through the branches unhurt to the ground. None of them suffered damage, apparently. But it certainly speaks for a constitution when an infant goes after life in this manner and gets away with it.

Bob-white has everything to recommend him. I should like to see him taken out of the game-bird class over all his range and made the special subject for study and honor. Hardy, friendly, musical, beneficial, he is by nature and habits our particular ally, a buffer spirit, or rather a go-between

> "In the primal sympathy
> Which, having been, must ever be"

linking all life together, men and quail.

We must have a yet friendlier mind for all outdoors. Conservation calls for knowledge as well as for sentiment. A marked sign of these times is the extent of our outdoor study, in school, out of school, among young and old, and persons of every sort. It has had much educat-

ing, and the mind of America is at last distinctly
inquiring and sympathetic toward all wild life,
though for many a wild form this knowledge and
interest has come too late. It finds these shapes
and races gone, their names forever blotted from
the Book of Life. For others, like the heath hen,
the California condor, the prong-horned antelope
of our sage plains, it has come in time to help,
and possibly to save.

All of this is a heavy price to pay for our dull
wits and savage hearts. Yet nothing less than
such irreparable loss could have aroused our
fears and conquered our desire to kill. The les-
son has gone none too deep even yet. See the
senseless wild-life slaughter going on in Africa,
sweeping that mighty continent like a fire. And
much of it by Americans, too! But over the
whole of America the slaughter still goes on in
spite of all that Americans have done in the way
of protection. Yet a great and beneficent work
has been started. Such far-reaching laws have
been enacted, such a new, wiser, kinder care sup-
plants the old spirit of slaughter, that we may
hope for a new earth, and such peace between
wild life and human life as only the poets and
prophets heretofore had dared to dream.

The bird-banding expedition down Cape Cod, which I described in a previous chapter, when registered aluminum bands were placed on the legs of 1,433 young black-crowned night herons, is an illustration of the newer hunting; the leader of the expedition before his conversion to the study of birds, had been a confirmed sportsman.

We do not need to band bob-white. His ways are known. The year around he will not wander farther than across the town. But as a game bird he is still a legal mark for the gunner. Time was when I have drawn a bead upon him as he rose from the stubble and scaled away on short spread wings over the old worm fence into the alder swale. It took time and honest thinking and self-denial to shift from gun to field-glasses, from shooting to watching, to know the difference between a frosty field with a living quail left in it, and that quail a bunch of bloody feathers in my game-bag.

We owe much good legislation to our sportsmen, no one wishes to deny that. But the plain fact remains that conditions for wild life have steadily and speedily changed for the worse, and that as matters stand, the sportsman who feeds and kills a covey of quail is not so good a conserver of birds as one who feeds them and lets them live.

And the clear sweet call from under the wall of the woods this morning proves how quickly, if given a chance, bob-white will return. Not since 1904 have native quail nested about Mullein Hill. They have from time to time been introduced here, and have strayed across from the sanctuary whistling until the gunning season in the fall. Then silence again.

One autumn lately I was slow getting up my "No GUNNING" signs, and the first day of open season on quail found me hastily nailing the notices along the public road. The sportsmen were ahead of me, shooting over the meadow on the opposite side of the road, following up the only covey in the neighborhood. There were two or three men and as many dogs. I knew my birds were finished.

Hurrying along with my warnings, I was driving a nail home when a gun spoke directly back of me, so close that I jumped as if I had been shot, and turning in my tracks saw a quail, wings wide open, head hanging, come up over the road and slide softly down at my feet, and at the foot of the maple tree under my futile sign!

The gunner approached and read my notice, looked down at the dead quail, and said: "I'm mighty sorry. It's the last of the covey, too. We've bagged 'em all." Then pointing to the "No GUNNING" sign, he went on, "Posting a little piece like yours won't do any good. We've got to post the whole country. But first we've got to be educated out of killing. I've shot all my life. It's hard to realize that a game bird does not belong to the man who can kill it according to law."

"You won't be shooting this way again this season?" I said.

"No. This is my one day off. And this is the last quail."

"But I'm living here all the time," I went on. "I've heard that quail calling throughout the summer, and there isn't a sweeter call, is there? You have killed him for an instant's excitement. I would have had the pleasure of hearing him for a year to come. I suppose you will eat him?"

"That's all he's good for dead," he replied, and picked up the bird, a beautiful male.

But the creature was not dead, not quite. Its body was paralyzed. A drop of blood was oozing from its conical beak. But its clear, beautiful eyes were wide open, as if for a last look upon the tinted woods and brown frosted fields of its home. There was no fear, no reproach, no sign of pain in the steady, gentle eyes. Death had laid his hand upon the wild thing and it was all soul. Pressing thumb and forefinger beneath the drooping wings the sportsman stopped the beating of the eager heart, dropped the exquisite creature into a canvas bag, and went his way.

I went my way, protesting—the open season, the pleasure of killing, and this swift, unfair, unprofitable doom.

CHAPTER THIRTEEN: A WORD MORE

THE MOON was up, the winter winds, too. We were returning home through the narrow wood-road when, as we swung into the driveway, the headlights picked out a half-dozen strange shapes under the lee of the stone wall. Fox hunters, bundled up against the weather, lying here out of the wind, listening to the baying of the hounds! The pack was a mile away among the quarries. No man of them had a gun—only the white moon, the scudding sky, the wind in the elms, and the far-off rise and fall of the baying, the elemental music of the chase.

These men were of all sorts, but all of them members of a local fox-hunting club, numbering, I have heard, more than a hundred strong. One trapper has caught twenty-three foxes this fall in this neighborhood, but he is not a member of the club. He may have killed the last one. Some day he will, and after that no more sweet baying of the pack beneath the watching moon, no line of sharp tracks across the snow, no lithe red form, keen faced, brushy tailed, trotting under my lower meadow bars!

Here is a fox club which has learned to hunt without a gun, else it could not hunt at all. A live fox in the woods is good hunting so long as he is alive. A gray goose honking down the sky is better sport than the same thing trussed upon a table.

Stop killing and start creating. Stop cutting and start planting. Stop wasting and start saving. Stop hunting and start watching. Stop hating and start loving. These are the ten commandments of conservation for each of us within his own dooryard and neighborhood, over his own ranch and farm; a sower of seed, a planter of trees, a nourisher of life, where heretofore we have each plucked and burned and slaughtered.

Whoever pollutes a stream poisons a people, no matter how many wheels the water turns, how many mouths the mill may feed. Mill-dam and fish-way can be built as one piece, a corporate part of a single undertaking for a life that is lovely, and a living that is more than bread.

For every stick of timber cut a seedling can be planted. And even if, in the wiser future, we can declare the open season on certain forms and in certain places, every thoughtful sportsman knows that today, should the shooting he desires for himself be claimed by us all, it would make a wild-life morgue of America before the pup he is training has been broken to the gun.

We still need legislation for the saving of wild life. Yet salvation is not in the law. It is in love. The law protects; the same law proscribes. We must abide by, but we dare not abide in, the law. Both right and wrong bear the name of the law. Love runs ahead of law, requires no law, and not only protects but plants and makes alive. We shall always need the law, but at this moment we need love infinitely more.

Let us enact conservation legislation at Washington. Meanwhile, in every schoolroom up and down the land, and across from shore to shore, let talk about birds and beasts and flowers and trees be started, let tramps afield be taken, and so, in every school-child's heart let love be planted, till knowledge of conservation be next to reading, writing and arithmetic, and love of nature next to love of God and neighbor. That for the future.

For the imperiled present what am I doing? And what is my town doing? You and your

town? Hingham has a three-thousand-acre Wild
Life Sanctuary, a Town Forest, an After-church
Field Club, a Garden Club, a chapter of the
D. A. R. making conservation a major theme,
and bee-keepers and bird-lovers not a few. And
I have a seven-acre woodlot, deeded in my name
and dedicated to trees and all wild neighbors; to
be willed to them, their heirs and assigns to grow
and nest and den thereon forever.

Seven all but useless acres that cost three hundred and fifty dollars—a year's fee for the country club! Seven acres in twenty-year-old growth
of gray birch, red and white oak, maple, ash,
hickory, flowering dogwood and pine! A rocky,
irregular piece, full of rabbit, skunk, and woodchuck dens! A piece that last season was a home
for one precious partridge nest, one cuckoo, one
turtle dove, and at least one red-eyed vireo!
Seven acres of growing trees, future timber, that
would have been felled last winter had I not ran-
somed them! Seven acres of thinning, trimming,
and trash-wood for kitchen stove and fireplace!
Seven acres of leafy shade, and leafy smells,
glorious in the spring with white dogwood, gorgeous with burnished colors in the autumn, and
lovely in every slender trunk and budded twig

standing etched against the wintry hillsides in the snow! Seven acres of work and watching and wealth—if joy is wealth, and health is wealth, and 6 per cent on your investment is wealth, which is a low rate to reckon the trash-wood returns! Seven acres left wild for all wild things —that is my small contribution. But oh, the difference to the landscape, to the woodchuck, and to me!

THE END